Beginning Angular with Typescript (covers Angular 6)

Greg Lim

THIRD EDITION: JULY 2018

Table of Contents

PREFACE

About this book

Angular is one of the leading frameworks to develop apps across all platforms. Reuse your code and build fast and high performing apps for any platform be it web, mobile web, native mobile and native desktop. You use small manageable components to build a large powerful app. No more wasting time hunting for DOM nodes!

In this book, we take you on a fun, hands-on and pragmatic journey to master Angular from a web development point of view. You'll start building Angular apps within minutes. Every section is written in a bite-sized manner and straight to the point as I don't want to waste your time (and most certainly mine) on the content you don't need. In the end, you will have what it takes to develop a real-life app.

As of the time of writing, this book is updated to cover Angular 6.

Requirements

Basic familiarity with HTML, CSS, Javascript and object-oriented programming

Contact and Code Examples

The source codes used in this book can be found in my GitHub repository at https://github.com/greglim81.

Please feel free to email me at support@i-ducate.com if you encounter any errors with your code or to get updated versions of this book.

Chapter 1: Introduction

1.1 What is Angular?

Angular is a framework for creating Single Page Applications (SPA). What is a Single Page Application? Most web applications are traditionally server-side applications. The server holds the business logic, stores data, and renders the website to the client. When a client clicks on a link, it sends a request to the server, and the server will handle this request and send back a response with html code which the browser will render and be viewed by the user.

The problem here is that with this approach, the server receives a lot of requests. For example, when we go to a website and click on its home page, we send a request for which the server has to respond. We click on the *About* page, and it sends another request, and the server responds. We click on *Blog*, and it sends another request, and again the server responds.

The many requests and response incur a lot of time and resources spent on these tasks which lead to a slow feeling of web pages. But whereas the apps on your mobile phone or desktop feel very fast most of the time. Angular wants to bring this app like feeling to the browser where we don't always have to load new pages each time there is an action from the user.

A user still clicks on various links in an SPA. However, this time, the client handles the requests on its own and will re-render the html page through Javascript, so the server is totally left out here if its possible that no data from the server is needed. This is much faster as we don't have to send any data over the internet, the client doesn't have to wait for the response, and the server doesn't have to render the response. Everything is done in the browser. Gmail is a good example of a SPA.

There are of course times when we need to get or send data from/to the server and we will need to send a request to the server. But these are restricted to initial loading and necessary server-side operations like database operations. Besides these operations, we will not need to request from the server. And even if we do need it, we do it asynchronously, which means we still re-render the page instantly to the user and then wait for the new data to arrive and incorporate it and render the view again when the data arrives.

This leads to a different set of requests. A typical request with a SPA page is the initial request to load the page when the user first visits the site. For the next request, however, when we visit the *About* page, we will not need to send a request to the server. Although we will need to send a request again when we visit the *Blog* page, we have already saved one request and a lot of time. And even when we do send requests, we still provide the instant reactive feeling to the user because we handle the response data asynchronously as we can instantly render the Blog page.

In this book, I will teach you about Angular from scratch in step by step fashion. It doesn't matter whether you are familiar with AngularJS (a.k.a. Angular 1) or not because Angular 6 (or simply 'Angular') is an entirely new framework. I will not be touching on AngularJS and how it is different from Angular because not every reader of this book is familiar with AngularJS and we do not want to distract you with the old way of development.

We will be using Typescript, a superset of Javascript for Angular development. Angular uses Typescript because its types make it easy to catch many programming errors during compile time.

In the course of this book, you will build an application where you can input search terms and receive the search results via GitHub RESTful api (fig. 1.1.2).

GitHub User Results

 gregkh
Score: 45.635616

 greg
Score: 44.03208

 gdb
Score: 38.98523

 gregheo
Score: 38.670673

figure 1.1.2

In the end, you will also build a real world application with full C.R.U.D. operations (fig. 1.1.3).

Users

Add

Username	Email	Edit	Delete
Ervin Howell	Shanna@melissa.tv	✓	✗
Clementine Bauch	Nathan@yesenia.net	✓	✗
Patricia Lebsack2	Julianne.OConner@kory.org2	✓	✗
Chelsey Dietrich	Lucio_Hettinger@annie.ca	✓	✗
Mrs. Dennis Schulist	Karley_Dach@jasper.info	✓	✗
Kurtis Weissnat	Telly.Hoeger@billy.biz	✓	✗

figure 1.1.3

These are the patterns you see on a lot of real-world applications. In this book, you will learn how to implement these patterns with Angular.

1.2 Architecture Overview of Angular Apps

The four main building blocks of an Angular app are modules, components, directives and services.

Modules

An Angular app is made up of separate modules which consist of closely related components of functionality. When we first begin creating our app, we will have only one module which is the root module AppModule. For small applications, the root module may be the only module. But most apps have multiple feature modules, each being groups of components that perform a role. For example, a social media app will have a post module, message module, followers module and so on.

Components

As mentioned, an Angular module is made up of components. For example, if we want to build a store front module like what we see on Amazon, we can divide it into three components. The search bar component, sidebar component and products component.

A component consists of an html template and a component class that has its own data and logic to control the html template. Components can also contain other components. In products component where we display a list of products, we do so by using multiple product components. Also, in each product component, we can have a rating component (fig. 1.2.1).

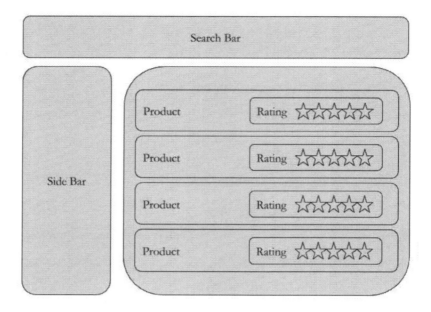

fig. 1.2.1

The benefit of such an architecture helps us to breakup a large application into smaller manageable modules, which in turn consists of smaller manageable components. Plus, we can reuse components within the application or even in a different application. For example, we can re-use the rating component in a different application.

Below is an example of a product component that allows users to specify a rating:

```
export class ProductComponent {
  rating;
  setRating(value){
    ...
  }
}
```

A component is simply a plain Typescript class like any other class that has properties and methods. The properties hold the data for the view and the methods implement the behavior of a view, like what should happen if I click a button.

Services

10

A service is a class with a well defined specific function that your application needs. For example, logging, talking to backend servers (e.g., Node, ASP.NET, Ruby on Rails) to get or save data, validating user input and so on.

Services provide their functionality to be consumed by components. Components should be light-weight, mainly rendering views through their template supported by application logic for better user experience. They don't fetch data from the server or validate user input but rather delegate such tasks to services.

Directives

Angular component templates are dynamic. When Angular renders them, it transforms the DOM according to the instructions given by directives. We use directives to alter the appearance or behavior of DOM elements. For example, we use the *autoGrow* directive to make the textbox automatically grow when it receives focus.

```
<input type="text" autoGrow />
```

Angular has a bunch of directives that alter the layout (e.g. *ngIf*), modify classes (*ngClass*) or styles (*ngStyles*) of DOM elements. You can also write your own custom directives.

This is the big picture for modules, components, services and directives. As you progress through this book, you will see each of these building blocks in action.

1.3 Setting Up

Installing Node

First, we need to install NodeJS. NodeJS is a server-side language, and we don't need it because we are not writing any server-side code. We mostly need it because of its *npm* or Node Package Manager. *npm* is very popular for managing dependencies of your applications. We will use npm to install other later tools that we need including Angular CLI.

Get the latest version of NodeJS from *nodejs.org* and install it on your machine. Installing NodeJS should be pretty easy and straightforward.

To check if Node has been properly installed, type the below on your command line (Command Prompt on Windows or Terminal on Mac):

```
node -v
```

and you should see the node version displayed.

To see if npm is installed, type the below on your command line:

```
npm -v
```

and you should see the npm version displayed.

Installing TypeScript

As explained, we will be using TypeScript for our Angular development. To install TypeScript, type the following command:

```
npm install -g typescript
```

or

```
sudo npm install -g typescript
```

if you are a Mac user.

With *-g* specified, we install TypeScript globally on our machine so that we can use it no matter which folder we navigate to. The same applies for our other installations.

Installing Typings

Once TypeScript is installed, we install Typings. Typings is a module that allows us to bring in Javascript libraries into TypeScript. We will learn more about it later. So in Command Prompt type

```
npm install -g typings
```
or `sudo npm install -g typings` for Mac users.

Installing Angular CLI

The Angular CLI is a *Command Line Interface* tool that makes creating a Angular project, adding files, and other on-going development tasks like testing, bundling and deployment easier.

To install Angular CLI from the command line, type

```
npm install -g @angular/cli
```

TypeScript Editor

Next, we need a code editor that supports TypeScript. In this book, I will be using VScode (https://code.visualstudio.com/) which is a good, lightweight and cross platform editor from Microsoft.

Chrome Browser

Finally, I will be using Chrome as my browser. You can use other browsers but I highly recommend you use Chrome as we will be using Chrome developer tools in this book and I want to make sure you have the same experience as we go through the coding lessons.

1.4 Creating a New Project with Angular CLI

First, navigate to the folder where you want to create your Angular project. Next, create a new Angular project and skeleton application with the following command (Note: ng refers to the Angular CLI tool),

```
ng new PROJECT_NAME
```

This will create your project folder and install everything you need to create your Angular application. Note that it takes time to set up a new project, most of it spent installing npm packages.

When the folder is created, navigate to it by typing.

```
cd PROJECT_NAME
```

Next, type

```
ng serve --open
```
node version 16.14.0

The above command launches the server, watches your files and rebuilds the app as you make changes to those files. Using the *--open* (or just *-o*) option will automatically navigate to http://localhost:4200/. Your app greets you with the message displayed in fig.1.4.1.

Welcome to app!!

fig. 1.4.1

Project File Review

Now let's look at the project files that have been created for us. When you open the project folder in VScode editor, you will find a couple of configuration files (fig. 1.4.2).

fig. 1.4.2

We will not go through all the files as our focus is to get started with our first Angular app quickly, but we will briefly go through some of the more important files and folders.

Our app lives in the *src* folder. All Angular components, templates, styles, images and anything else our app needs goes here. Any other files outside of this folder are meant to support building your app (the app folder is where we will work 99% of the time!). In the course of this book, you will come to appreciate the uses for the rest of the configuration files.

In the *src* folder, we have *main.ts* which is the main entry point for our app. It compiles the application with the JIT compiler and bootstraps the applications's root module AppModule to run in the browser.

tsconfig.json is the Typescript compiler configuration for our app. i.e., how to compile our TypeScript files into Javascript.

package.json is the node package configuration which lists the third party packages our project uses. You can also add custom scripts here.

node_modules folder is created by Node.js and puts all third party modules listed in *package.json* in it.

In the *app* folder, we find a couple of other TypeScript files:

app.module.ts is the root module that tells Angular how to assemble our application. As mentioned earlier, an Angular application comprises of separate modules which are closely related blocks of functionality. Every Angular application has at least one module: the root module, named AppModule here. For many small applications, the root module AppModule alone is enough. For bigger modules, we can create multiple modules. We will illustrate this in **Chapter 11 - Structuring Large Apps With Modules**.

```typescript
import { BrowserModule } from '@angular/platform-browser';
import { NgModule } from '@angular/core';
import { FormsModule } from '@angular/forms';
import { HttpClientModule } from '@angular/common/http';

import { AppComponent } from './app.component';

@NgModule({
  declarations: [
    AppComponent
  ],
  imports: [
    BrowserModule,
    FormsModule,
    HttpClientModule
  ],
  providers: [],
  bootstrap: [AppComponent]
})
export class AppModule { }
```

A module is a class with the *@NgModule* decorator. Angular has decorators that attach metadata to classes so that it knows what those classes are and how they should work. For example, modules and components have decorators that tell Angular that they are modules and components respectively. The *@NgModule* decorator is a function that takes a single metadata object whose properties describe the module. The most important properties are:

declarations - to declare which components, directives or pipes belong to this module. For now, it is just AppComponent. But we will soon start adding other components to this array.

exports – to specify which components should be visible and useable by other modules *imports* - to specify what other modules whose exported classes are needed by components declared in this module. Angular comes with pre-defined modules like the *BrowserModule, FormsModule and HttpClientModule.* As a brief introduction, the *BrowserModule* contains browser related functionality. It also contains the common module which has *ngIf, ngFor* which we will introduce later. The FormsModule is needed when working with input fields and other forms related functionality. The HttpClientModule is needed when working with http access.

Since our application is a web application that runs in a browser, the root module needs to import the BrowserModule from *@angular/platform-browser* to the *imports* array. For now, our application doesn't do anything else, so you don't need any other modules. In a real application, you'd likely import FormsModule and HttpClientModule, and that is why we keep it there.

providers - to specify any application wide services we want to use

app.component.ts

```
import { Component } from '@angular/core';

@Component({
  selector: 'app-root',
  templateUrl: './app.component.html',
  styleUrls: ['./app.component.css']
})
export class AppComponent {
  title = 'app works!';
}
```

Every Angular application has at least one component: the root component named AppComponent in *app.component.ts.* Components are the basic building blocks of Angular applications. A component controls a portion of the screen, a view - through its associated html template, *app.component.html. app.component.css* is the css file referenced from *app.component.ts*

We define our component's application logic (what it does to support the view) inside a class. The class interacts with the view through properties and methods. For now, our root app component class has only a variable *title*.

This class is decorated with the Component decorator *@Component.* Like the module decorator, the component decorator adds metadata above this class. Because decorators are functions, we need to use the prefix @ sign to call the *@Component* function with its brackets *@Component(...).* All components in Angular are essentially decorated TypeScript classes.

```
@Component({
  selector: 'app-root',
  templateUrl: './app.component.html',
```

16

```
  styleUrls: ['./app.component.css']
})
```

1.5 Editing our first Angular Component

The CLI created the first Angular component for us. This is the root component located in *app.component.ts*.

Now open app.component.ts and change the title property to *My First Angular App* as shown below.

```
export class AppComponent {
  title = 'My First Angular App!';
}
```

Notice that the browser reloads automatically with the revised title because TypeScript compiler is running in the 'watch' mode, it detects that there is a file change and re-compiles the file. In the Chrome browser, the app gets refreshed automatically, so you don't have to refresh the page every time your code changes.

How does the title get rendered? The html markup of our component is stored in *app.component.html* which has the following code

```
<h1>
  Welcome to {{title}}!!
</h1>
```

With {{*title*}} we are using string interpolation which we will explore this in detail later. But basically, this allows you to output any property of your component dynamically into the html. So {{*title*}} here actually refers to the *title* property in our *app.component.ts*.

Summary

In this chapter, we have been introduced to the core building blocks of Angular apps which are components, directives, services and routers. We have also been introduced to the Angular development experience which is coding in TypeScript and having TypeScript compiler automatically generate our app for us that we can view on the browser. In the next chapter, we will begin implementing an Angular app.

CHAPTER 2: CREATING AND USING COMPONENTS

In the previous chapter, you learned about the core building blocks of Angular apps, components, directives, services and modules. In this chapter, we will implement a component, directive and service from scratch to have an idea of what it is like to build an Angular app.

2.1 Creating our First Component

In VScode, open the project folder that you have created in chapter 1. We first add a new file in the app folder and call it *products.component.ts*.

Note the naming convention; we start with the name of the component *products* followed by *component.ts*. Remember that *ts* stand for TypeScript.

Type out the below code into *products.component.ts*:

```
import { Component } from '@angular/core'

@Component({
    selector: 'products',
    template: '<h2>Products</h2>'
})
```

```
export class ProductsComponent{

}
```

Code Explanation

import { Component } from '@angular/core' imports the component decorator from the *core* Angular module.

The component decorator *@Component* tells Angular that this class is going to be a component.

The *@Component* function takes in a metadata object {} with 2 attributes, *selector* and *template* both of type string as shown below:

```
@Component({
    selector: 'products',
    template: '<h2>Products</h2>'
})
```

selector property tells Angular to display the component inside a custom *<products>* tag in *index.html*.

template specifies the html inline that will be inserted into the DOM when the component's view is rendered. We can either write the html here inline or define the template in a separate html file with the *templateUrl* property. Our current html markup is *<h2>Products</h2>*.

Lastly, the *export* keyword makes this class available for other files in our application to import this class.

With these simple lines of code, we have just built our first component!

2.2 Using our Created Component

Now, go back to *app.component.ts*. Notice that the contents of *app.component.ts* are very similar to *products.component.ts*.

```
import { Component } from '@angular/core';

@Component({
  selector: 'app-root',
  templateUrl: './app.component.html',
  styleUrls: ['./app.component.css']
})
export class AppComponent {
  title = 'My First Angular App';
}
```

To re-iterate, we import the component decorator, *import { Component } from '@angular/core';*

We then call it using *@Component()* and give it an object with fields, *selector, templateUrl* and *styleUrls*. With the field *templateUrl*, we refer to our html markup in a separate file *app.component.html*. When the html markup is big, it is better to put it in a separate file using *templateUrl*. However, if the html markup is not too big, it is easier to have it in the *component.ts* file as we can view it all at a single glance. Let's do this now by changing *templateUrl* to *template* and inserting our html markup in *app.component.ts*. Change your code to the below:

```
import { Component } from '@angular/core';

@Component({                  ⟵ changed from templateUrl
  selector: 'app-root',
  template: '<h1>{{title}}</h1>',
  styleUrls: ['./app.component.css']
})
export class AppComponent {
  title = 'My First Angular App';
}
```

The same applies for the *styleUrls* attribute, which refers to *app.component.css* as the css file. Because *app.component.css* is currently empty, and we have no use of it yet, we can just remove that attribute to make the code cleaner as in below (remember to remove the comma at the end of the template line):

```
import { Component } from '@angular/core';

@Component({
  selector: 'app-root',
  template: '<h1>{{title}}</h1>'
})
export class AppComponent {
  title = 'My First Angular App';
}
```

At this point, we can delete *app.component.html* and *app.component.css* file.

Lastly, we export this component in *export class AppComponent*. Remember that App component is the root of our application. It is the view component that controls our entire app or page.

Now, add *<products></products>* to the template as shown below.

```
import { Component } from '@angular/core';

@Component({
  selector: 'app-root',
```

```
  template:
    `<h1>{{title}}</h1>
    <products></products>`
})
export class AppComponent {
  title = 'My First Angular App';
}

export class AppComponent { }
```
typo? already exporting

*Do note that the slashes used in the `template` attribute is the **backtick** character `` ` ``. The backtick `` ` `` is located in the top left of the keyboard just before the number 1. The backtick allows us to put html markup into multiple lines therefore making our template more readable.

app.module.ts

Next, edit the file *app.module.ts* to import your new ProductsComponent and add it in the declarations array in the *NgModule* decorator (see below code in **bold**). Because ProductsComponent is added to the declarations array of AppModule, AppComponent does not have to import ProductsComponent again since we have specified that AppComponent and ProductsComponent belong to the same module and therefore have access to one another.

```
import { BrowserModule } from '@angular/platform-browser';
import { NgModule } from '@angular/core';
import { FormsModule } from '@angular/forms';

import { AppComponent } from './app.component';

import { ProductsComponent }   from './products.component';

@NgModule({
  declarations: [
    AppComponent, ProductsComponent
  ],
  imports: [
    BrowserModule,
    FormsModule,
  ],
  providers: [],
  bootstrap: [AppComponent]
})
export class AppModule { }
```

Save the file and go to your browser. You should see the Products component markup displayed with the message:

My First Angular App'.

Products

Code Explanation

We first import our *ProductsComponent* using

```
import { ProductsComponent }   from './products.component';
```

For custom components that we have defined, we need to specify their path in the file system. Since App component and ProductsComponent are in the same folder app, we use './' which means start searching from the current folder followed by the name of the component, *products.component* (without *.ts* extension).

When we add *ProductsComponent* to the *declarations* array, we are saying that it is part of this module. So when Angular sees the *<products>* tag, Angular will know that ProductsComponent is responsible for that.

```
template:
  <h1>{{title}}</h1>
  <products></products>
```

<products></products> here acts as a custom directive. Remember that a directive is a class that allows us to extend or control our Document Object Model. In this way, we can design custom elements that are not part of standard html. In our case, we use the ProductsComponent to define a new element.

How is our Root Component Rendered?

Our root component's template is defined as

```
@Component({
  selector: 'app-root',
  template:
    `<h1>{{title}}</h1>
    <products></products>`
})
```

<app-root> is rendered because in *index.html* (shown below in **bold**), the element <app-root> is referenced in <body>. Angular saw this, instantiates an instance of AppComponent and rendered it inside the <app-root> tag.

```
<html>
<head>
  <meta charset="utf-8">
  <title>Angular2Firstapp</title>
  <base href="/">

  <meta name="viewport" content="width=device-width, initial-scale=1">
  <link rel="icon" type="image/x-icon" href="favicon.ico">
</head>
<body>
  <app-root>Loading...</app-root>
</body>
</html>
```

→ 2.3 Component Templates

We define a component's view with its companion template. A template is a form of html that tells Angular how to render the component. We can define properties and display them in the template. For example, App component has a property *title* which holds the value 'My First Angular App'.

```
export class AppComponent {
  title = 'My First Angular App';
}
```

Note that Angular can automatically infer the type of the variable by the value assigned to it. But we can explicitly set the type of the variable (if we want to) as shown below.

```
title: string = 'My First Angular App';
```

Interpolation

The value of *title* is rendered on to our template with double curly braces {{*title*}}.

```
  template:
    `<h1>{{title}}</h1>
    <products></products>`
```

This is called interpolation. If the value of this property in the component changes, the view will be automatically refreshed. This is called one-way binding (where the value displayed in the html markup is binded to the component's property). We also have two-way binding which is used in forms. For example, when we type something into an input field that is bound to a property, as you modify the value of the input field, the component's property will be updated automatically. You will see that later in the Forms chapters (six and seven).

Displaying a List with *ngFor

We will illustrate using properties further by displaying a list of products in ProductsComponent. First, we declare an array *products* in ProductsComponent which contains the names of the products that we are listing.

```
export class ProductsComponent{
    products = ["Learning Angular","Pro TypeScript","ASP.NET"];
}
```

goes after the @ Component declaration not before (handwritten annotation)

Next in the template, we use `<ul>` and `<li>` to render the list of products.

```
@Component({
    selector: 'products',
    template: `
        <h2>Products</h2>
        <ul>
            <li *ngFor="let product of products">
                {{product}}
            </li>
        </ul>
    `
})
```

Navigate to your browser and you should see the result in fig. 2.3.1

My Second Angular App

Products

- Learning Angular 2
- Pro TypeScript
- ASP.NET

fig. 2.3.1

Code Explanation

<li *ngFor="let product of products"> duplicates the *<li></li>* for each product in the list. The **ngFor* keyword acts like a for-loop, setting the *product* temporary local variable to the product item in the current iteration.

For each product, we use interpolation {{*product*}} to display the product.

A template looks like regular html except for a few differences. Code like *ngFor* is an example of a directive provided by Angular. This directive extends the html and adds extra behavior, in this case, repeating the <*li*> element based on the expression assigned to it.

2.4 Services

Currently, our component is rendering a hardcoded list of products. We would instead need to get data from a server. As mentioned earlier, components should only contain logic related to the view. Logic to get data from a server should not be in a component but instead be encapsulated in a separate class called a **service**. We will now create a service that will simulate getting data from a server.

In the app folder, create a new file called product.service.ts. Note the naming convention, we start with the name of the service and then '.service.ts'. Type in the below code into 'product.service.ts'.

```
export class ProductService{
    getProducts() : string[] {
        return ["Learning Angular","Pro TypeScript","ASP.NET"];
    }
}
```

Code Explanation

If you notice, a service (like a component) is just a plain class. It contains a method *getProducts()* of return type *string array* as represented by *getProducts() : string[]*. For now, we illustrate by returning the same hard-coded array as before so as not to get distracted by how to call a RESTful api in our service (we will do that later in chapter 8 and 9).

2.5 Dependency Injection

Back in products.component.ts, change the code to below.

```
import { Component } from '@angular/core'
import { ProductService } from './product.service'

...

export class ProductsComponent{
    products;

    constructor(productService: ProductService){
        this.products = productService.getProducts();
```

```
    }
}
```

Code Explanation

The constructor populates our string array *products*. The constructor takes in a ProductService object. We call the *getProducts()* method of the ProductService object and assign the results to our products array.

But how do we create the *Product* service and pass it into the constructor? The answer is Dependency Injection. Dependency injection supplies *instances* of your classes that you depend on. Most dependencies classes are Services. Angular can tell which services a component needs by looking at the types of its constructor parameters. For example, the constructor of ProductsComponent needs a Product Service. So when Angular creates a ProductsComponent, it looks at the constructor and see that we need a ProductService, it will create an instance of ProductService and then inject it into the constructor of the ProductsComponent class.

providers

Lastly, in app.component.ts, add the lines in **bold**.

```
import { Component } from '@angular/core';

import { ProductService } from './product.service';

@Component({
  selector: 'app-root',
  template:
    `<h1>{{title}}</h1>
    <products></products>`,
  providers: [ProductService]
})
export class AppComponent {
  title: string = 'My First Angular App';
}
```

The providers array contain the dependencies of the ProductsComponent. So here, we say that ProductService is a dependency of ProductsComponent. In general, add providers to the root module so that the same instance of a service is available everywhere.

If you run the application now, you should see the same list of products as before. Only now that we have encapsulated the data retrieval logic to ProductService and ensure that ProductsComponent contains only user-interface related logic.

Summary

You have learnt a lot in this chapter. If you get stuck while following the code or if you would like to get the sample code we have used in this chapter, visit my GitHub repository at https://github.com/greglim81 or contact me at support@i-ducate.com.

In this chapter, we briefly looked at Components, Directives, Services and Dependency Injection. We have created a ProductsComponent that retrieves product data through a Service, and later displays that data on the page.

CHAPTER 3: BINDINGS

In this chapter, we will explore displaying data by binding controls in an html template to properties of an Angular component, how to apply css classes on styles dynamically and how to handle events raised from DOM elements.

3.1 Property Binding

We have learnt about interpolation where we display a property of a component in the view through putting the property name in double curly braces for example, *<h1>{{title}}</h1>*.

Another example of property binding is binding the image element to a component's *imageUrl* property. In the existing project from chapter two, change the code in app.component.ts as shown below:

app.component.ts

```
import { Component } from '@angular/core';

@Component({
  selector: 'app-root',
  template: `
    <h1>{{title}}</h1>
    <img src="{{imageUrl}}" />
    `
})
export class AppComponent {
  title = 'My First Angular App';
  imageUrl = "https://www.w3schools.com/html/pic_mountain.jpg";
}
```

3.2 CSS Class Binding

In the below code, we show a button in our view using two bootstrap css classes *btn* and *btn-primary* to make our button look more professional. Bootstrap is a html, css, javascript framework that contains html and css based templates to help build user interface components (like forms, buttons, icons) for web applications.

```
@Component({
  selector: 'app-root',
```

```
template: `
  <button class="btn btn-primary">Submit</button>
  `
})
```

We first however need to reference bootstrap.css in our index.html. Go to getbootstrap.com and under 'Getting Started', copy the below *bootstrap.min.css* stylesheet link:

```
<link rel="stylesheet"
href="https://maxcdn.bootstrapcdn.com/bootstrap/3.3.7/css/bootstrap.min.c
ss">
```

and paste the link into index.html as shown below in **bold**. For this chapter, we will be using bootstrap version 3.3.7 (see below) because version 4 of bootstrap no longer offers glyphicons.

```
<html>
<head>
  <meta charset="utf-8">
  <title>Angular2Firstapp</title>
  <base href="/">

  <meta name="viewport" content="width=device-width, initial-scale=1">
  <link rel="icon" type="image/x-icon" href="favicon.ico">
  <link rel="stylesheet"
href="https://maxcdn.bootstrapcdn.com/bootstrap/3.3.7/css/bootstrap.min.c
ss">
</head>
<body>
  <app-root>Loading...</app-root>
</body>
</html>
```

If you have successfully linked your bootstrap class, you should get your button displayed like in fig. 3.2.2.

fig. 3.2.2

There are times when we want to use different css classes on an element based on different conditions. For example, if I want to disable the button by applying the *disabled* class, I can do the following

30

```
@Component({
  selector: 'app-root',
  template: `
    <button
      class="btn btn-primary"
      [class.disabled]="!isValid">Submit</button>
    `
})
export class AppComponent {
  isValid = false;
}
```

That is, when *isValid = false* the disabled css class will be applied making the button unclickable. If *isValid = true* the disabled css class will not be applied making the button clickable.

3.3 Binding to User Input Events

We can use event binding to respond to any DOM event. Many DOM events are triggered by user input. Binding to these events provides a way to get input from the user.

To bind to a DOM event, surround the event name in parentheses and assign a quoted template statement to it like in the example below.

```
@Component({
  selector: 'app-root',
  template: `
    <button (click)="onClickMe($event)">Submit</button>
    `
})
export class AppComponent {
  onClickMe($event) {
    console.log("Clicked",$event)
  }
}
```

The *(click)* to the left of the equals sign identifies the button's click event as the target event to be binded. "onClick()" in quotes is the template statement which responds to the click event by calling the components onClickMe method.

DOM events carry a payload of information that maybe useful to the component. The *$event* argument in *onClickMe($event)* allows us to get access to the event raised. For example, in keystrokes, the event object can tell us the user's input after each keystroke. The properties of an *$event* object vary depending on the type of DOM event. For example, a mouse event includes different information from an input box editing event. Note that there is a *$* prefix in *$event* because this is built into Angular. The *event*

31

object is a standard DOM event object and has got nothing to do with Angular.

There is one more kind of binding called two way binding which we will explore later in our Forms chapter.

3.4 Example Application

We will now put into practice what we have learnt about data binding. We will build a rating component like in figure 3.4.1.

★ ★ ★ ★ ☆

fig. 3.4.1

You have seen such a rating component in many places e.g. Amazon. So we can implement this as a component and reuse it in many places. A user can click select from a rating of one star to five stars. For now, don't worry about calling a server or any other logic. We just want to implement the UI.

Open the existing project folder from chapter two, create a new component class rating.component.ts and fill it with the below code.

```typescript
import { Component } from '@angular/core'

@Component({
    selector: 'rating',
    template: `
        <i
            class="glyphicon"
            [class.glyphicon-star-empty]="rating < 1"
            [class.glyphicon-star]="rating >= 1"
            (click)="onClick(1)"
        >
        </i>
        `
})
export class RatingComponent{
    rating = 0;

    onClick(ratingValue){
        this.rating = ratingValue;
    }
}
```

Next in app.module.ts, import the rating component and add it to the *declarations* array by adding the below lines in **bold**. By adding RatingComponent to *declarations*, we specify that it is part of AppModule and can therefore be used in AppComponent.

```
import { ProductsComponent } from './products.component';
import { RatingComponent } from './rating.component';

import { ProductService } from './product.service';

@NgModule({
  declarations: [
    AppComponent, ProductsComponent, RatingComponent
  ],
  imports: [
    BrowserModule,
    FormsModule,
  ],
  //providers: [ProductService],
  providers: [],
  bootstrap: [AppComponent]
})
export class AppModule { }
```

Lastly, in app.component.ts, add the *<rating>* element in the template as shown below:

```
import { Component } from '@angular/core';

@Component({
  selector: 'app-root',
  template: `
    <rating></rating>
    `
})
export class AppComponent {
    title = "hello";
}
```

Code Explanation

```
@Component({
    selector: 'rating',
    template: `
        <i
            class="glyphicon"
            [class.glyphicon-star-empty]="rating < 1"
            [class.glyphicon-star]="rating >= 1"
            (click)="onClick(1)"
        >
        </i>
```

```
})
```

We define a component called Rating Component with selector as *'rating'* so in app.component.ts, we create an instance of it with **<rating></rating>.**

In the template, we render bootstrap glyphicons using *class="glyphicon"* and use class binding to conditionally render a secondary class with:

```
[class.glyphicon-star-empty]="rating < 1"
[class.glyphicon-star]="rating >= 1"
```

(Although bootstrap 4.0.0 no longer supports glyphicons, you can get the available complete list of glyphicons from https://getbootstrap.com/docs/3.3/components/.)

The condition is based on the property *rating* defined in the RatingComponent class below.

```
export class RatingComponent{
    rating = 0;

    onClick(ratingValue){
        this.rating = ratingValue;
    }
}
```

The condition works like the following; if the rating is less than one, we render the empty star icon.
```
[class.glyphicon-star-empty]="rating < 1"
```

If the rating is more than or equal to one, we render the normal star icon.
```
[class.glyphicon-star]="rating >= 1"
```

We add a click handler *(click)="onClick(1)"* to assign a rating of one if a user clicks on this star.

You would probably notice that we have only one star at this point, when ratings usually have five stars. This is because I wanted you to be familiar with the logic of one star. To then extend it to five stars is easy. Simply copy and paste the glyphicon code in the template for additional stars as shown below.

```
@Component({
    selector: 'rating',
    template: `
        <i
            class="glyphicon"
            [class.glyphicon-star-empty]="rating < 1"
            [class.glyphicon-star]="rating >= 1"
            (click)="onClick(1)"
```

```
        >
        </i>
        <i
            class="glyphicon"
            [class.glyphicon-star-empty]="rating < 2"
            [class.glyphicon-star]="rating >= 2"
            (click)="onClick(2)"
        >
        </i>
        <i
            class="glyphicon"
            [class.glyphicon-star-empty]="rating < 3"
            [class.glyphicon-star]="rating    >= 3"
            (click)="onClick(3)"
        >
        </i>
        <i
            class="glyphicon"
            [class.glyphicon-star-empty]="rating < 4"
            [class.glyphicon-star]="rating >= 4"
            (click)="onClick(4)"
        >
        </i>
        <i
            class="glyphicon"
            [class.glyphicon-star-empty]="rating < 5"
            [class.glyphicon-star]="rating >= 5"
            (click)="onClick(5)"
        >
        </i>
        `
})
```

Note that you need to do two things. Firstly, change the value of each condition depending on which star it is. The second star's condition should be

```
[class.glyphicon-star-empty]="rating < 2"
[class.glyphicon-star]="rating >= 2"
```

The second star should be empty if the rating is less than two. It should be filled if the rating is more than or equal to two. The same goes for the third, fourth and fifth star.

Secondly, change the value of the argument when you called the *onClick* method depending on which star it is. The second star's *onClick* should be *(click)="onClick(2)"*. So when a user clicks on the second star, the *onClick* method is called with property *rating* of value two. When a user clicks on the third star, the *onClick* method is called with property *rating* of value three and so on.

35

Summary

In this chapter, you learnt about property binding, class binding, style binding, event binding, and two-way binding. In the next chapter, we will take a closer look at Angular components.

Visit my GitHub repository at https://github.com/greglim81 if you have not already to have the full source code for this chapter or contact me at support@i-ducate.com if you encounter any errors with your code.

CHAPTER 4: WORKING WITH COMPONENTS

In this chapter, we will learn more about using components, how to reuse them and put them together in an application. Execute the codes in the following sections in your existing project from chapter three.

4.1 Input Properties

We can mark properties in our component as *input* or *output* properties. Properties marked as *input* or *output* will be visible from the outside and available for property or event binding. For example, in our button element, we can bind its *value* property to a property in our component.

```
<button [value] = "title" (click)="onClick($event)">Submit</button>
```

value here is an example of an *input* property. We can use it to pass data to our button. Buttons also have events like *(click)* that we can bind to methods in our components. *(click)* is an example of an output property.

We can also define the *input* and *output* properties for a custom component. Suppose we want to display a list of products with its rating. We will need to assign the rating value to our rating component beforehand. However, we currently can only use our rating component like this *<rating></rating>*.

If we want to do something like, *<rating [rating]="4"></rating>* to display a rating of 4 stars, we have to declare our component property *rating* with the *@Input* decorator.

To declare an input property, first in *rating.component.ts*, we need to import *Input* (see code in **bold** below).

```
import { Component, Input } from '@angular/core'
```

Next, add the `@Input()` decorator before the property as shown below.

```
@Component({
    selector: 'rating',
    template: `
        ...
    `
})
export class RatingComponent{
    @Input() rating = 0;

    onClick(ratingValue){
```

```
        this.rating = ratingValue;
    }
}
```

4.2 Styles

With the *styles* property, you can define css styles required by your component (or in a separate file(s) with *styleUrls*). These *styles* are scoped only to your component. They won't effect to the outer html or other components.

To illustrate, suppose we want our filled glyphicon stars to be orange, we add the following in **bold**.

```
@Component({
    selector: 'rating',
    templateUrl: 'rating.component.html',
    styles: [`
        .glyphicon-star {
            color: orange;
        }
    `]
})
```

When we run our application, we will see our filled stars with the orange css applied to it.

★ ★ ★ ★ ☆ Submit

4.3 Example Application

We will reuse the rating component that we have made and implement a product listing like in figure 4.3.1.

Products

Product 1

May 31, 2016 ★ ★ ★ ★ ☆ 2

Cras sit amet nibh libero, in gravida nulla. Nulla vel metus scelerisque ante sollicitudin commodo. Cras purus odio, vestibulum in vulputate at, tempus viverra turpis. Fusce condimentum nunc ac nisi vulputate fringilla. Donec lacinia congue felis in faucibus.

Product 2

May 31, 2016 ★ ★ ★ ★ ☆ 12

Cras sit amet nibh libero, in gravida nulla. Nulla vel metus scelerisque ante sollicitudin commodo. Cras purus odio, vestibulum in vulputate at, tempus viverra turpis. Fusce condimentum nunc ac nisi vulputate fringilla. Donec lacinia congue felis in faucibus.

Product 3

May 31, 2016 ★ ★ ★ ★ ★ 245

Cras sit amet nibh libero, in gravida nulla. Nulla vel metus scelerisque ante sollicitudin commodo. Cras purus odio, vestibulum in vulputate at, tempus viverra turpis. Fusce condimentum nunc ac nisi vulputate fringilla. Donec lacinia congue felis in faucibus.

fig. 4.3.1

This is like the list of products on Amazon. For each product, we have an image, the product name, the product release date, the rating component and the number of ratings it has.

In the project folder, create a new component file *product.component.ts* that contain ProductComponent. This component will be used to render one product. Fill in the file with the below code.

```
import {Component, Input} from '@angular/core';

@Component({
    selector: 'product',
    template: `
    `,
    styles: [`
        .media {
            margin-bottom: 20px;
        }
    `]
})
export class ProductComponent {
    @Input() data;
}
```

39

Now, how do we get our template to render each product listing like in figure 4.4.1? We use the media object in bootstrap. Go to getbootstrap.com, in the **components** page, click on media object and copy the markup there into the template field of ProductComponent.

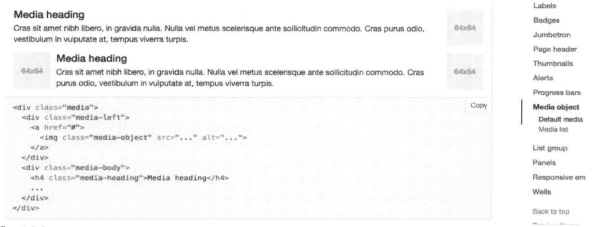

fig. 4.3.2

Next in the template, we use interpolation to assign values of our product into the DOM. Type in the below codes in bold into the template.

```
@Component({
    selector: 'product',
    template: `
        <div class="media">
            <div class="media-left">
                <a href="#">
                <img class="media-object" src="{{ data.imageUrl }}">
                </a>
            </div>
            <div class="media-body">
                <div class="media-body">
                    <h4 class="media-heading">
                        {{ data.productName }}
                    </h4>
                    {{ data.releasedDate }}
                    <rating
                        [rating-value]="data.rating"
                        [numOfReviews]="data.numOfReviews">
                    </rating>
                    <br>
                    {{ data.description }}
                </div>
```

40

```
            </div>
        </div>
    `,
    styles: [`
        .media {
            margin-bottom: 20px;
        }
    `]
})
```

With the above code, our product component is expecting a data object with the fields: *imageUrl*, *productName*, *releasedData* and *description*.

We have also added our rating component that expects input rating and number of reviews.

```
<rating
        [rating-value]="data.rating"
        [numOfReviews]="data.numOfReviews">
</rating>
```

Our rating component currently only has *rating-value* as input. Add the below code in **bold** into rating.component.ts to add *numOfReviews* as input.

```
import { Component, Input } from '@angular/core'

...
export class RatingComponent{
    @Input('rating-value') rating = 0;
    @Input() numOfReviews = 0;

    onClick(ratingValue){
        this.rating = ratingValue;
    }
}
```

Also add {{ *numOfReviews* }} at the end of rating.component.html to display the number of reviews beside the rating stars.

Next, we create a new file product.service.ts that contains a service class ProductService that is responsible for returning a list of products. Type in the below code into ProductService class.

```
export class ProductService{
    getProducts() {
        return [
        {
            imageUrl: "http://loremflickr.com/150/150?random=1",
```

```
            productName: "Product 1",
            releasedDate: "May 31, 2016",
            description: "Cras sit amet nibh libero, in gravida... ",
            rating: 4,
            numOfReviews: 2
        },
        {
            imageUrl: "http://loremflickr.com/150/150?random=2",
            productName: "Product 2",
            releasedDate: "October 31, 2016",
            description: "Cras sit amet nibh libero, in gravida... ",
            rating: 2,
            numOfReviews: 12
        },
        {
            imageUrl: "http://loremflickr.com/150/150?random=3",
            productName: "Product 3",
            releasedDate: "July 30, 2016",
            description: "Cras sit amet nibh libero, in gravida... ",
            rating: 5,
            numOfReviews: 2
        }];
    }
}
```

Notice that in our class, we currently hardcode an array of product objects. Later on, we will explore how to receive data from a server.

For *imageUrl*, we use http://loremflickr.com/150/150?random=1 to render a random image 150 pixels by 150 pixels. For multiple product images, we change the query string parameter *random=2, 3,4* and so on to get a different random image.

Just like before, the *getProducts* method in ProductService will be called by ProductsComponent. The code remains largely the same (see below) and that is the benefit for having separation of concerns to have data retrieving functionality (non UI related) in a separate service class rather than in a component.

```
import { Component } from '@angular/core'
import { ProductService} from './product.service'

@Component({
    selector: 'products',
    template: `
            <h2>Products</h2>
            <div *ngFor="let product of products">
                <product [data]="product"></product>
```

```
        </div>
        `,
    providers: [ProductService]
})
export class ProductsComponent{
    products;

    constructor(productService: ProductService){
        this.products = productService.getProducts();
    }
}
```

The *ngFor* loops through products array as retrieved from ProductService and inputs each data element in the products array for each product component. Each data element provides Product component with values from properties *imageUrl*, *productName*, *releasedData* and *description*.

We also import ProductService and declare it in the *providers* array to specify that we depend on ProductService as a service provider.

Lastly in app.module.ts in the lines in **bold** below, we import ProductComponent and add it to the *declarations* array to declare ProductComponent as part of AppModule.

```
import { BrowserModule } from '@angular/platform-browser';
import { NgModule } from '@angular/core';
import { FormsModule } from '@angular/forms';

import { AppComponent } from './app.component';

import { ProductsComponent } from './products.component';
import { ProductComponent } from './product.component';
import { RatingComponent } from './rating.component';

import { ProductService } from './product.service';

@NgModule({
  declarations: [
    AppComponent, ProductsComponent, RatingComponent, ProductComponent
  ],
  imports: [
    BrowserModule,
    FormsModule
  ],
  providers: [],
  bootstrap: [AppComponent]
})
export class AppModule { }
```

43

Save all your files and you should have your application running fine like in figure 4.3.3.

Products

Product 1

May 31, 2016 ★ ★ ★ ★ ☆ 2

Cras sit amet nibh libero, in gravida nulla. Nulla vel metus scelerisque ante sollicitudin commodo. Cras purus odio, vestibulum in vulputate at, tempus viverra turpis. Fusce condimentum nunc ac nisi vulputate fringilla. Donec lacinia congue felis in faucibus.

Product 2

May 31, 2016 ★ ★ ★ ★ ☆ 12

Cras sit amet nibh libero, in gravida nulla. Nulla vel metus scelerisque ante sollicitudin commodo. Cras purus odio, vestibulum in vulputate at, tempus viverra turpis. Fusce condimentum nunc ac nisi vulputate fringilla. Donec lacinia congue felis in faucibus.

Product 3

May 31, 2016 ★ ★ ★ ★ ★ 245

Cras sit amet nibh libero, in gravida nulla. Nulla vel metus scelerisque ante sollicitudin commodo. Cras purus odio, vestibulum in vulputate at, tempus viverra turpis. Fusce condimentum nunc ac nisi vulputate fringilla. Donec lacinia congue felis in faucibus.

figure 4.3.3

Summary

In this chapter, we illustrate how to define input properties in a component, use both inline templates and templates defined in a separate file with *templateUrl*, use styles to define css styles used in a component and borrow markup from *bootstrap* to put all these together in our example Product Listing application.

Contact me at support@i-ducate.com if you encounter any issues or visit my GitHub repository at https://github.com/greglim81 for the full source code of this chapter.

CHAPTER 5: CONDITIONAL RENDERING, PIPES AND NG-CONTENT

We have worked with *ngFor* which is one of the built in directives in Angular. In this chapter, we will explore more built in directives which will give us more control in rendering html.

5.1 ngIf

Suppose you want to show or hide part of a view depending on some condition. For example, we have earlier displayed our list of products. But if there are no products to display, we want to display a message like "No products to display" on the page.

In products.component.ts of the existing project from chapter four, add the codes in **bold**

```
import { Component } from '@angular/core'
import { ProductService} from './product.service'

@Component({
    selector: 'products',
    template: `
            <h2>Products</h2>
            <div *ngIf="products.length > 0">
                <div *ngFor="let product of products">
                    <product [data]="product"></product>
                </div>
            </div>
            <div *ngIf="products.length == 0">
                No products to display
            </div>

            `,
    providers: [ProductService]
})
export class ProductsComponent{
    products;

    constructor(productService: ProductService){
        this.products = productService.getProducts();
    }
}
```

45

Now when we run our app again, we should see the products displayed as same as before. But if we comment out our hard-coded data in ProductService and return an empty array instead, we should get the following message.

Products

No products to display

Code Explanation

```
<div *ngIf="products.length > 0">
    <div *ngFor="let product of products">
        <product [data]="product"></product>
    </div>
</div>
```

We used the *ngIf* directive to add a if-condition in our DOM and assign an expression *"products.length > 0"* to it. If the expression evaluates to true, the *div* element and its children will be inserted into the DOM. If it evaluates to false, it will be removed from the DOM. When there are products returned from ProductService, the expression evaluates to true and renders the products in the *ngFor* loop.

The following expression however evaluates to false and therefore, we don't display the message.

```
<div *ngIf="products.length == 0">
    No products to display
</div>
```

When we return an empty array however, *"products.length > 0"* evaluates to false and we do not render the list of products. Instead we display the "No products to display" message.

ngIfElse

As of Angular 4, there is an improved *ngIf* which supports an if/else syntax. The above code can be implemented with if/else like the below:

```
<h2>Products</h2>
<div *ngIf="products.length == 0; else loading">
    No products to display
</div>
<ng-template #loading>
```

```
    <div *ngIf="products.length > 0">
        <div *ngFor="let product of products">
            <product [data]="product"></product>
        </div>
    </div>
</ng-template>
```

Code Explanation

```
    <div *ngIf="products.length == 0; else loading">
        No products to display
    </div>
```

The above code is saying, "If products array length is 0, then show this current div and anything inside of it. Otherwise (else) show the *ng-template* named #loading.

5.2 ngSwitch

In a similar fashion as *ngIf*, the *ngSwitch* statement allows us to render elements and its children based on a condition against a list of values.

Suppose we want to add a comment based on the product rating as in figure 5.2.1,

Products

Product 1

May 31, 2016 ★ ★ ★ ★ ☆ 2

Very Good

Cras sit amet nibh libero, in gravida nulla. Nulla vel metus sceler
odio, vestibulum in vulputate at, tempus viverra turpis. Fusce co
Donec lacinia congue felis in faucibus.

Product 2

October 31, 2016 ★ ★ ☆ ☆ ☆ 12

Fair

Cras sit amet nibh libero, in gravida nulla. Nulla vel metus sceler
odio, vestibulum in vulputate at, tempus viverra turpis. Fusce co
Donec lacinia congue felis in faucibus.

Product 3

July 30, 2016 ★ ★ ★ ★ ★ 2

Excellent

Cras sit amet nibh libero, in gravida nulla. Nulla vel metus sceler
odio, vestibulum in vulputate at, tempus viverra turpis. Fusce co
Donec lacinia congue felis in faucibus.

fig. 5.2.1

where one star means 'Poor', two star - 'Fair', three star - Good, four star - 'Very Good', five star -
'Excellent'. We can achieve this by adding the below code in **bold** into the *template* field of
product.component.ts.

```
template: `
    <div class="media">
        <div class="media-left">
            <a href="#">
            <img class="media-object" src="{{ data.imageUrl }}">
            </a>
        </div>
        <div class="media-body">
            <h4 class="media-heading">
                {{ data.productName }}
            </h4>
            {{ data.releasedDate }}
            <rating
                [rating-value]="data.rating"
                [numOfReviews]="data.numOfReviews">
            </rating>
            <div [ngSwitch]="data.rating">
```

```
            <div *ngSwitchCase="1">Poor</div>
            <div *ngSwitchCase="2">Fair</div>
            <div *ngSwitchCase="3">Good</div>
            <div *ngSwitchCase="4">Very Good</div>
            <div *ngSwitchCase="5">Excellent</div>
            <div *ngSwitchDefault>Not Rated</div>
        </div>
        <br>
        {{ data.description }}
    </div>
</div>
`,
```

So depending on the value of *data.rating*, we display different product comments. We use **ngSwitchDefault* in the case where the value of *data.rating* does not match any of the cases; we display a default message 'Not Rated'.

5.3 Pipes

To format data in Angular, we can use 'pipes'. A pipe takes in data as input and transforms it into the desired output. Angular has built in pipes like *DatePipe*, *UpperCasePipe*, *LowerCasePipe*, *CurrencyPipe*, and *PercentPipe*. We can also create custom pipes which we will visit in the next section. Because pipes are relatively straightforward, we will illustrate the *DatePipe* and you can go on to explore the rest of the built in pipes on your own.

First, we change the value of *releasedDate* in the object returned by ProductService to a Javascript *Date* object as shown in bold below.

```
return [
{
    imageUrl: "http://loremflickr.com/150/150?random=1",
    productName: "Product 1",
    releasedDate: new Date(2016,5,30),
    description: "...",
    rating: 4,
    numOfReviews: 2
},
```

We have assigned *releasedDate* with a *Date* object with value 30 Jun, 2016. (Note that the month count starts from 0). Now, the date gets displayed as "Thu Jun 30 2016 00:00:00 GMT+0800 (SGT)" which is not what we want to display to the user. To use pipe formatting, in product.component.ts, we do the below,

```
{{ data.releasedDate | date }}
```

The date now gets displayed as Jun 30, 2016.

Parameterizing a Pipe

We can also supply pipes with optional parameters to fine tune its format. We do so by adding a colon (:) and then the parameter value (e.g., date:"MM/dd/yy"). The below code returns our date 06/30/16 in the specified format of MM/dd/yy.

```
{{ data.releasedDate | date:"MM/dd/yy" }} // 06/30/16
```

Chaining Pipes

We can also chain pipes together for useful combinations. In the below example, we chain *releasedDate* to *DatePipe* and on to *UpperCasePipe* to display the date in uppercase. The following birthday displays as JUN 30, 2016.

```
{{ data.releasedDate | date | uppercase }} // JUN 30, 2016
```

5.4 Custom Pipes

We can also write our own custom pipes. We use custom pipes the same way we use built-in pipes. We will implement a custom pipe that takes a string and truncate it to a specified length. This is useful for displaying a truncated product description in the view if it is too long like in figure 5.4.1.

Products

Product 1

Jun 30, 2016 ★ ★ ★ ★ ☆ 2

Very Good

Cras sit amet nibh libero, in gravida nulla. Nulla...

Product 2

Nov 30, 2016 ★ ★ ☆ ☆ ☆ 12

Fair

Cras sit amet nibh libero, in gravida nulla. Nulla...

Product 3

Aug 30, 2016 ★ ★ ★ ★ ★ 2

Excellent

Cras sit amet nibh libero, in gravida nulla. Nulla...

fig. 5.4.1

First, create a new file truncate.pipe.ts in the app folder. Type in the below codes into the file.

```
import { Pipe, PipeTransform } from '@angular/core';

@Pipe({name: 'truncate'})

export class TruncatePipe implements PipeTransform {
    transform(value: string, limit:number): string{
        return value.substring(0,limit) + "...";
    }
}
```

Code Explanation

A pipe is a plain TypeScript class decorated with pipe metadata *@Pipe({name: 'truncate'})*. We tell Angular this is a pipe by applying the *@Pipe* decorator which we import from the *core* Angular library. The *@Pipe* decorator allows us to define the pipe name that we'll use within template expressions. Our pipe's name is *truncate*.

Every pipe class implements the *PipeTransform* interface's transform method. The *transform* method accepts an input *value* followed by optional parameters and returns the transformed value. In our code, *value* is the string we want to truncate and *limit* determines the limit of our truncation.

```
export class TruncatePipe implements PipeTransform {
    transform(value: string, limit:number): string{
        return value.substring(0,limit) + "...";
    }
}
```

Final Steps

Next, we have to include our pipe in the *declarations* array of the AppModule to specify that our pipe is part of the AppModule. Add the lines below in **bold** to app.module.ts.

```
import { BrowserModule } from '@angular/platform-browser';
...
...
import { RatingComponent } from './rating.component';

import { TruncatePipe } from './truncate.pipe';

@NgModule({
  declarations: [
    AppComponent, ProductsComponent, RatingComponent, ProductComponent,
TruncatePipe
  ],
  imports: [
      ...
  ],
  providers: [],
  bootstrap: [AppComponent]
})
export class AppModule { }
```

Finally in product.component.ts, add the pipe to the *data.description* interpolation like,
{{ *data.description* | *truncate: 20*}}

5.5 ng-content

Sometimes, we need to insert content into our component from the outside. For example, we want to implement a component that wraps a bootstrap jumbotron. A bootstrap jumbotron (fig. 5.6.1) as defined on getbootstrap.com is "A lightweight, flexible component that can optionally extend the entire viewport to showcase key content on your site."

Hello, world!

This is a simple hero unit, a simple jumbotron-style component for calling
extra attention to featured content or information.

Learn more

fig. 5.5.1

Here is an implementation of the bootstrap jumbotron component.

```
import { Component, Input } from '@angular/core';

@Component({
  selector: 'bs-jumbotron',
  template: `
   <div class="jumbotron">
     <p></p>
     <p><a class="btn btn-primary btn-lg" href="#" role="button"></a></p>
   </div>
`
})
export class JumboTronComponent {
}
```

The markup above can be obtained from http://getbootstrap.com/components/#jumbotron.

The selector is *bs-jumbotron*. We add a prefix *bs-* ('bs' as an abbreviation for bootstrap) to distinguish this component from other components that potentially might have the same name. The jumbotron component is called in app.component.ts using,

```
import { Component } from '@angular/core';

@Component({
  selector: 'app-root',
  template: `
    <bs-jumbotron></bs-jumbotron>
`
})
```

```
export class AppComponent {
}
```

To supply content to the jumbotron component, we can use *Input* properties. We can define an Input property in our jumbotron component and use property binding as shown below:

```
<bs-jumbotron [body]="..."></bs-jumbotron>
```

This is not ideal, however, for we probably want to write a lengthier html markup here like,

```
<bs-jumbotron>
    This is a simple hero unit, a simple jumbotron-style component for
calling extra attention to featured content or information.
</bs-jumbotron>
```

We want to insert content into the jumbotron component from the outside. To do so, we define insertion points with *ng-content* as shown below into our jumbotron component template.

```
@Component({
  selector: 'bs-jumbotron',
  template: `
    <div class="jumbotron">
      <p><ng-content></ng-content></p>
      <p><a class="btn btn-primary btn-lg" href="#" role="button"></a></p>
    </div>
  `
})
export class JumboTronComponent {
}
```

This is a simple hero unit, a simple jumbotron-style component for calling extra attention to featured content or information.

Multiple Insertion Points

We can also define multiple insertion points by adding the select directive. In bs-jumbotron.component.ts, we do this by using *ng-content* and specifying a css class to the *select* attribute to distinguish where content should go.

```
import { Component, Input } from '@angular/core';

@Component({
```

```
    selector: 'bs-jumbotron',
    template: `
      <div class="jumbotron">
          <h1><ng-content select=".heading"></ng-content></h1>
          <p><ng-content select=".body"></ng-content></p>
          <p><a class="btn btn-primary btn-lg" href="#" role="button">
              <ng-content select=".button"></ng-content></a></p>
      </div>
`
})
export class JumboTronComponent {
}
```

In the above code, we specify that content with the class heading will be placed in the h1 heading tag. Content with class body will be placed in the body and content with class *button* will be in the button.

We now add in app.component.ts the rest of the text with the various css classes as shown below.

```
@Component({
    selector: 'app-root',
    template: `
      <bs-jumbotron>
        <div class="heading">
          Hello World!
        </div>
        <div class="body">
          This is a simple hero unit, a simple jumbotron-style component for
calling extra attention to featured content or information.
        </div>
        <div class="button">
          Learn more
        </div>
      </bs-jumbotron>
      `
})
export class AppComponent {
}
```

If you run your app now, you should now see something like in figure 5.6.2.

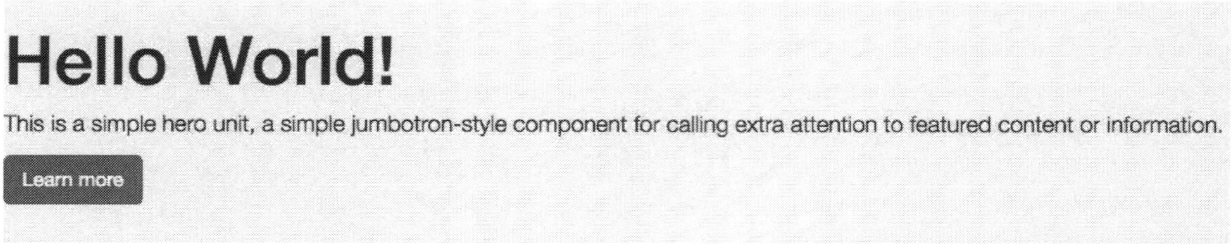

Hello World!

This is a simple hero unit, a simple jumbotron-style component for calling extra attention to featured content or information.

fig. 5.5.2

Summary

In this chapter, we introduced built in directives like *ngFor*, *ngIf* and *ngSwitch* that gives us more control in rendering our html. We learnt about formatting data using built in pipes like DatePipe, UpperCasePipe and creating our own custom pipes for custom formatting. We have also learnt about inserting content into components from the outside using *ng-content*.

Contact me at support@i-ducate.com if you encounter any issues or visit my GitHub repository at https://github.com/greglim81 for the full source code of this chapter.

CHAPTER 6: TEMPLATE DRIVEN FORMS

In Angular, we have template driven and model driven forms. Template driven forms are easier to implement and involve writing less code. But they give us limited control over validation. Model driven forms have more code, but we have full control over validation. In this chapter, we will look at template driven forms.

6. 1 Create the User Model Class

Before we create our form, we want to define a class or model that can hold the data that we receive from the form. A model is represented by a simple class that contains properties. We will create a User class with two required fields (first name, email) and one optional field (country).

Create a new Angular project (using Angular CLI) and in the *app* folder, create a new file called user.ts with the following code:

```
export class User {
  constructor(
    public firstName: string,
    public email: string,
    public country?: string
  ) {  }
}
```

Note that the *?* in country specifies that it's an optional field.

Next, create a new file called user-form.component.ts and give it the following definition:

```
import { Component } from '@angular/core';
import { User }     from './user';

@Component({
  selector: 'user-form',
  templateUrl: 'user-form.component.html'
})
export class UserFormComponent {
    countries = ['United States', 'Singapore',
                 'Hong Kong', 'Australia'];

    model = new User('','','');
```

```
    submitted = false;

    onSubmit() {
        this.submitted = true;
    }
}
```

In the UserFormComponent, we import the *User* model we just created. We specify our selector to be *user-form*. Because the html markup will be quite long, we use the *templateUrl* property to point to a separate html file user-form.component.html for our template.

6.2 Revising app.module.ts

Because template-driven form features are in FormsModule, we need to add it to the imports array in app.module.ts if we have not already done so. FormsModule gives our application access to template-driven forms features, including *ngModel*.

We also import the UserFormComponent and add it to *declarations* array in app.module.ts so that UserFormComponent is accessible throughout this module.

*Note: I was initially confused on whether a component should be in the *imports* or *declarations* array. The simple rule is, if a component, directive, or pipe belongs to a module in the *imports* array, don't declare it in the *declarations* array. If you wrote a component and it should belong to this module, do declare it in the *declarations* array.

6.3 Create an initial HTML Form Template

Next, create our template file user-form.component.html and give it the following definition:

```
<div class="container">
    <h1>User Form</h1>
    <form>
      <div class="form-group">
        <label for="firstName">First Name</label>
        <input type="text" class="form-control" id="firstName" required>
      </div>
      <div class="form-group">
        <label for="email">Email</label>
        <input type="text" class="form-control" id="email" required>
      </div>
      <div class="form-group">
        <label for="country">Country</label>
        <input type="text" class="form-control" id="country">
```

```
    <select class="form-control" id="country">
       <option *ngFor="let c of countries" [value]="c">{{c}}</option>
    </select>
  </div>
  <button type="submit" class="btn btn-default">Submit</button>
</form>
</div>
```

Our form definition till now is just plain html5. We are not using Angular yet. We allow *firstName* and *email* fields for user input in input boxes. Both *firstName* and *email* have the html5 *required* attribute; the *country* does not have *required* because it is optional.

At the end we have a *Submit* button.

6.4 Using *ngFor to Display Options

In the *country* field, we choose one country from a fixed list of countries using the *select* dropdown. We will retrieve the list of countries from an array in UserFormComponent and bind the options to the country list using *ngFor* with the below code.

```
<div class="form-group">
  <label for="country">Country</label>
  <select class="form-control" id="country">
     <option *ngFor="let c of countries" [value]="c">{{c}}</option>
  </select>
</div>
```

With **ngFor*, we repeat the *<option>* tag for each country in the list of countries. The variable *c* holds a different country element in each iteration and we display it using interpolation {{*c*}}.

6.5 Two-way data binding with ngModel

We use *[(ngModel)]* to easily create two way binding between our form and the *User* model.

Now, update *<input>* for *firstName* like this

```
<div class="form-group">
  <label for="firstName">First Name</label>
  <input type="text" class="form-control" id="firstName" required
      [(ngModel)]="model.firstName" name="firstName">
</div>
```

We have also added a name attribute to our <input> tag and set it to *firstName*. We can assign any unique

value, but we should use a descriptive name like the name of the input.
The *name* attribute is required by Angular Forms to register the control with the form.

Do the same for the rest of the fields as in below.

```
<div class="container">
    <h1>User Form</h1>
    <form>
      <div class="form-group">
        <label for="firstName">First Name</label>
        <input type="text" class="form-control" id="firstName" required
            [(ngModel)]="model.firstName" name="firstName">
      </div>
      <div class="form-group">
        <label for="email">Email</label>
        <input type="text" class="form-control" id="email" required
            [(ngModel)]="model.email" name="email">
      </div>
      <div class="form-group">
        <label for="country">Country</label>
        <select class="form-control" id="country"
            [(ngModel)]="model.country" name="country">
          <option *ngFor="let c of countries" [value]="c">{{c}}</option>
        </select>
      </div>
      <button type="submit" class="btn btn-default">Submit</button>
    </form>
</div>
```

Note that the *id* property in each input or select is used by the label to match to its attribute so that when a user clicks on the label, the input or select receives the focus, therefore enabling better user interaction since a user can either click on the label or input itself for the right focus.

If we run the application now, we should get something like in figure 6.5.1.

User Form

First Name

Greg

Email

greg@gmail.com

Country

Singapore

Submit

figure 6.5.1

6.6 Track change-state and validity with ngModel

ngModel not only provide us with two-way data binding between the form and controls, it also allows us to track change state and validity of the controls. This is useful to let us know if an input has been filled in and if the input is valid so that we can display alert or warning messages to the user.

For a control with *ngModel* directive, if a user has touched the control, the control's Angular css class *ng-touched* returns true and *ng-untouched* returns false. The reverse is true.
If the value of the control is changed, its *ng-dirty* class returns true and *ng-pristine* returns false. The reverse is true.
If the value of the control is valid, *ng-valid* class returns true and *ng-invalid* returns false. The reverse is true.

In the following, we illustrate how to make use of these css classes to display alert or warning messages when an input is improperly filled in.

Show and Hide Validation Error messages

In the below code, we first add the *#firstName* variable and give it the value ngModel to create a reference to the *firstName* input control so that we can access its css classes. Next, we show the "First Name is required" message if *firstName.touched* is true and *firstName.valid* is false. Note that we have divided the markup of the input element into multiple lines instead of one single line so that it is easier to see its attributes.

```
<div class="form-group">
  <label for="firstName">First Name</label>
```

61

```
<input type="text"
    class="form-control"
    id="firstName" required
    [(ngModel)]="model.firstName"
    name="firstName"
    #firstName="ngModel"
>
<div class="alert alert-danger"
    *ngIf="firstName.touched && !firstName.valid ">
    First name is required
</div>
</div>
```

Why do we check *touched?* This is to avoid showing errors before the user has had a chance to edit the value, for example when the form is freshly loaded. This prevents premature display of errors.

We proceed to do the same for *email* input.

```
<div class="form-group">
  <label for="email">Email</label>
  <input type="text"
      class="form-control"
      id="email" required
      [(ngModel)]="model.email"
      name="email"
      #email="ngModel">
  <div *ngIf="email.touched && !email.valid"
      class="alert alert-danger">Email is required.
  </div>
</div>
```

We don't show or hide any validation messages for *country* since it is optional so we leave it as it is.

6.7 Showing Specific Validation Errors

Other than the required validation, we can also specify our input validation on an element's minimum and maximum length using its *minlength* and *maxlength* html validation attributes. The below code illustrates this.

```
<div *ngIf="firstName.touched && firstName.errors">
    <div class="alert alert-danger"
        *ngIf="firstName.errors.required">
        First name is required
    </div>
    <div class="alert alert-danger"
```

```
        *ngIf="firstName.errors.minlength">
        First name should be minimum 3 characters.
    </div>
  </div>
```

The first *ngIf* on the outer *<div>* element reveals two nested message *divs* if the control is touched and there are *firstName* errors.

Inside the outer *<div>* are two nested *<div>* which presents a custom message for *required* and *minlength* validation error.

6.8 Submit the form with ngSubmit

To implement submitting of forms, we update the <form> tag with the Angular directive NgSubmit and bind it to the UserFormComponent.submit() method with an event binding in the below code.

```
<form (ngSubmit)="onSubmit()" #userForm="ngForm">
```

In the <form> tag, we also define a variable #userForm and assign the value "ngForm" to it to make *userForm* a reference to the form as a whole. The *ngForm* directive allows *userForm* to hold control to its contained elements with the *ngModel* directive and name attribute. *userForm* thus allows us to monitor these contained control elements' properties including their validity. *userForm* also has its own valid property which is true only if every contained control is valid. This enables us to bind the *Submit* button's disabled property to the form's over-all validity via the *#userForm* variable. That is, the *Submit* button remains disabled until all required inputs are filled up properly. We do this with the below code in the *Submit* button.

```
<button type="submit" class="btn btn-default"
        [disabled]="!userForm.form.valid">Submit</button>
```

Now when either *firstName* or *email* field is not filled up, the error is shown and the *Submit* button is disabled.

6.9 Getting Submitted Values

To show that we have successfully submitted our form with its values, add the below code to the bottom of user-form.component.html.

```
<div [hidden]="!submitted">
  You submitted the following:
  First Name: {{ model.firstName }}<br>
  Email: {{ model.email }}<br>
  Country: {{ model.country }}<br>
```

```
<button class="btn btn-default"
    (click)="submitted=false">Remove</button>
</div>
```

When we click submit, we display the values entered with interpolation bindings (fig. 6.9.1). The values only appears while the component is in the submitted state. We added a *Remove* button whose click event sets *submitted* to false which removes the values.

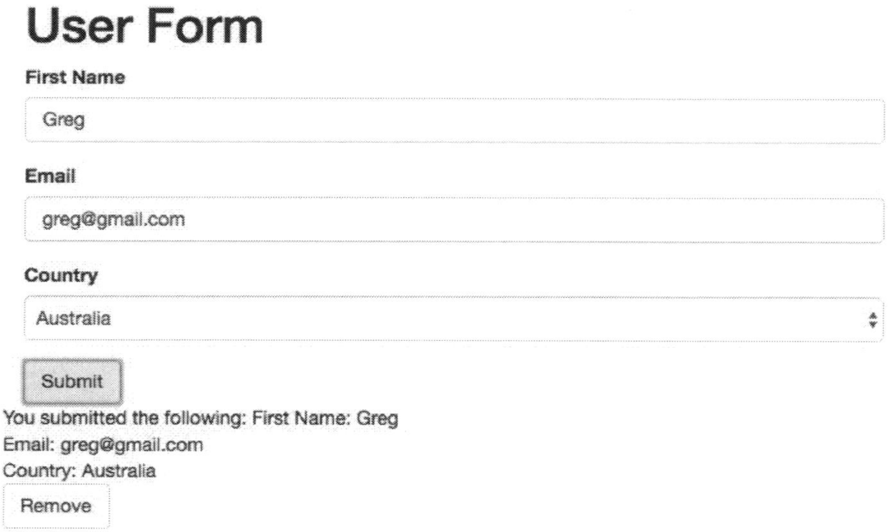

User Form

First Name

Greg

Email

greg@gmail.com

Country

Australia

Submit

You submitted the following: First Name: Greg
Email: greg@gmail.com
Country: Australia

Remove

fig. 6.9.1

Here is the final code of user-form.component.html

```
<div class="container">
    <h1>User Form</h1>
    <form (ngSubmit)="onSubmit()" #userForm="ngForm">
      <div class="form-group">
        <label for="firstName">First Name</label>
        <input type="text"
            class="form-control"
            id="firstName" required
            [(ngModel)]="model.firstName"
            name="firstName"
            #firstName="ngModel"
            minlength="3">
        <!-- display validation error-->
        <div *ngIf="firstName.touched && firstName.errors">
            <div class="alert alert-danger"
```

64

```
                *ngIf="firstName.errors.required">
                First name is required
        </div>
        <div class="alert alert-danger"
                *ngIf="firstName.errors.minlength">
                First name should be minimum 3 characters.
        </div>
      </div>
    </div>
    <div class="form-group">
      <label for="email">Email</label>
      <input type="text"
          class="form-control"
          id="email" required
          [(ngModel)]="model.email"
          name="email"
          #email="ngModel"
          minlength="3">
      <!-- display validation error-->
      <div *ngIf="email.touched && email.errors">
          <div class="alert alert-danger"
                *ngIf="email.errors.required">
                Email is required
          </div>
          <div class="alert alert-danger"
                *ngIf="email.errors.minlength">
                Email should be minimum 3 characters.
          </div>
      </div>
    </div>
    <div class="form-group">
      <label for="country">Country</label>
      <select class="form-control" id="country"
          [(ngModel)]="model.country" name="country">
          <option *ngFor="let c of countries"
                [value]="c">{{c}}</option>
      </select>
    </div>
    <button type="submit" class="btn btn-default"
          [disabled]="!userForm.form.valid">Submit</button>
  </form>
</div>
<div [hidden]="!submitted">
  You submitted the following:
  First Name: {{ model.firstName }}<br>
  Email: {{ model.email }}<br>
  Country: {{ model.country }}<br>
```

```
    <button class="btn btn-default"
(click)="submitted=false">Remove</button>
</div>
```

Here is the final code of user-form.component.ts

```
import { Component } from '@angular/core';
import { User }     from './user';

@Component({
  selector: 'user-form',
  templateUrl: 'user-form.component.html'
})
export class UserFormComponent {
    countries = ['United States', 'Singapore',
                 'Hong Kong', 'Australia'];

    model = new User('','','');

    submitted = false;

    onSubmit() {
        this.submitted = true;
    }
}
```

Summary

In this chapter, we learnt how to create a template driven form. We created a model class to represent the data in the form, used *ngFor* to display the list of options in a *select* dropdown, created two-way binding with form and component properties using *ngModel*, used *ngModel* to help us show form field validation errors, and finally learnt form submission using *ngSubmit*.

CHAPTER 7: MODEL DRIVEN FORMS

In the previous chapter, we learn about template driven forms. With template driven forms however, we are limited to a few basic validators. If we want to implement custom validation, we need to use model driven forms which we will cover in this chapter.

7.1 Building a Basic Login Form

We will first create a component that renders a simple login form. Create a new Angular project (remember to add the bootstrap link in index.html)and in *app*, create a new file login.component.ts with the below code.

```
import { Component } from '@angular/core';

@Component({
    selector:'login',
    templateUrl: 'login.component.html'
})
export class LoginComponent  {

}
```

Next create login.component.html as referenced in *templateUrl* property in login.component.ts. Fill in login.component.html with the below code.

```
<form>
    <div class="form-group">
        <label for="username">Username</label>
        <input id="username" type="text" class="form-control">
    </div>
    <div class="form-group">
        <label for="password">Password</label>
        <input id="username" type="password" class="form-control">
    </div>
    <button class="btn btn-primary" type="submit">Login</button>
</form>
```

The template above is currently just pure html with a few bootstrap classes. It does not have any validation or any Angular directives yet. In the next few sections, we will upgrade our form and implement custom validation on the username and password field.

7.2 Creating Controls Explicitly

To upgrade our form into an Angular form that can perform validation, we have to create *FormControl* and *FormGroup* objects. A FormControl object represents a form control in a form. With it, we can track the value and validation status of an individual form control. A FormGroup object tracks the value and validity state of a *group* of FormControl objects.

In login.component.ts, add the codes in **bold** shown below.

```
import { Component } from '@angular/core';
import { FormGroup, FormControl } from '@angular/forms';

@Component({
    selector:'login',
    templateUrl: 'login.component.html'
})
export class LoginComponent  {
    form = new FormGroup();
}
```

We have created a property called *form* and initialize it with *new FormGroup()*. FormGroup and FormControl are imported from *angular/forms*.

We next pass in two FormControl objects, *username* and *password* into FormGroup(). as show below.

```
import { Component } from '@angular/core';
import { FormGroup, FormControl, Validators } from '@angular/forms';

@Component({
    selector:'login',
    templateUrl: 'login.component.html'
})
export class LoginComponent  {
    form = new FormGroup({
        username: new FormControl ('', Validators.required),
        password: new FormControl ('', Validators.required)
    });
}
```

The first parameter in the FormControl constructor is optional. It is the default value we give to the control. This is useful when we display existing data in the control for user to edit. We first retrieve the existing value from the server and populate the control with it.

The second parameter takes in a *Validator* function. *Validators* is defined in *angular/commons* and provides a set of validators like *required*, *minlength* and *maxlength*. For now, we have used *Validators.required*.

Back in the template, we need to tell Angular that we have created a *FormGroup* and its *FormControls* explicitly so that Angular will not create them for us as in the case of template driven forms.

In login.component.html, add the codes in **bold**.

```
<form [formGroup]="form">
    <div class="form-group">
        <label for="username">Username</label>
        <input id="username" type="text" class="form-control"
            formControlName="username">
    </div>
    <div class="form-group">
        <label for="password">Password</label>
        <input    id="username"    type="password"    class="form-control"
            formControlName="password">
    </div>
    <button class="btn btn-primary" type="submit">Login</button>
</form>
```

Code Explanation

```
<form [formGroup]="form">
```

In the form element, we apply the *formGroup* directive and bind it to "form".

```
        <input id="username" type="text" class="form-control"
            formControlName="username">
```

We then associate each input field to the FormControl object by using *formControlName* directive formControlName="username". This is important for referencing our FormControl object from FormGroup. Angular will look at the FormGroup object and expects to find the FormControl object with the exact name we specify in formControlName="username". If it can't find the control with that name, it will throw an exception.

Implementing Validation

Next, we define validation message placeholders that will be displayed when the input is invalid. Add the following codes in **bold**.

```
<form [formGroup]="form">
    <div class="form-group">
        <label for="username">Username</label>
        <input type="text" class="form-control"
            formControlName="username">
        <div *ngIf="form.controls.username.touched &&
```

69

```
        !form.controls.username.valid" class="alert alert-danger">
            Username is required
        </div>
    </div>
    <div class="form-group">
        <label for="password">Password</label>
        <input type="password" class="form-control"
            formControlName="password">
        <div *ngIf="form.controls.password.touched &&
            !form.controls.password.valid" class="alert alert-danger">
            Password is required
        </div>
    </div>
    <button class="btn btn-primary" type="submit">Login</button>
</form>
```

Code Explanation

We check *username* css classes *touched* and *valid* to see if the control has been touched and input value is not valid. If so, display the div validation placeholder message "Username is required" with *alert* and *alert-danger* bootstrap classes. We do the same for password (figure 7.2.1).

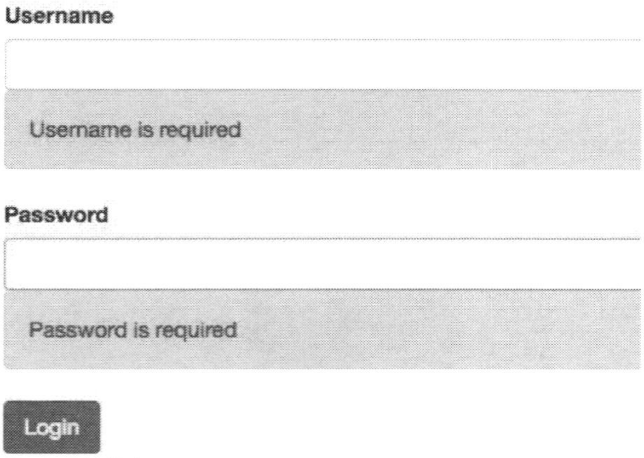

figure 7.2.1

Submitting the Form

To handle the *submit* event of the form, bind the ngSubmit event to the login() method in the *form* element as shown below.

```
<form [formGroup]="form" (ngSubmit)="login()">
```

70

Now in login.component.ts, we implement the login method.

```
export class LoginComponent  {
    form = new FormGroup({
        username: new FormControl ('', Validators.required),
        password: new FormControl ('', Validators.required)
    });

    login(){
        console.log(this.form.value); // prints form values in json format
    }
}
```

login() currently just prints the submitted values in json format.

app.component.ts

Next in app.component.ts, render the *login* component in the template:

```
import { Component } from '@angular/core';

@Component({
  selector: 'app-root',
  template: `
    <login></login>
    `
})
export class AppComponent {
}
```

Lastly in app.module.ts, import ReactiveFormsModule and add it to the *imports* array as shown below. ReactiveFormsModule provides the classes for implementing model driven forms.

```
import { BrowserModule } from '@angular/platform-browser';
import { NgModule } from '@angular/core';
import { ReactiveFormsModule } from '@angular/forms';

import { AppComponent } from './app.component';
import { LoginComponent } from './login.component';

@NgModule({
  declarations: [
    AppComponent,
  ],
  imports: [
    BrowserModule,
```

71

```
      ReactiveFormsModule
  ],
  providers: [],
  bootstrap: [AppComponent]
})
export class AppModule { }
```

What we have covered so far for model driven forms (e.g. Validation) is similar to template driven forms. The difference is that in model driven forms we are explicitly creating FormGroup and FormControl objects explicitly (in template driven forms, Angular creates it for you), and we tell Angular about it in the template by using the formGroup and formControlName directive.

7.3 Using FormBuilder

We can use the FormBuilder class to declare FormControl and FormGroup objects in a more compact way. For example, the previous form can also be implemented with FormBuilder as shown below.

```
import { Component } from '@angular/core';
import { FormBuilder, FormGroup, FormControl, Validators } from
'@angular/forms';

@Component({
    selector:'login',
    templateUrl: 'login.component.html'
})
export class LoginComponent  {

    form: FormGroup;

    constructor(fb: FormBuilder){
        this.form = fb.group({
            username:['',Validators.required],
            password:['',Validators.required]
        })
    }

    login(){
        console.log(this.form.value);
    }
}
```

Code Explanation

```
import { FormBuilder, FormGroup, FormControl, Validators } from
'@angular/forms';
```

We first import the FormBuilder class from @angular/forms. Because we are no longer using FormControl class, we can remove it from the import.

```
form: FormGroup;

constructor(fb: FormBuilder){
    this.form = fb.group({
        username:['',Validators.required],
        password:['',Validators.required]
    })
}
```

In the constructor, we use dependency injection to get an instance of FormBuilder, fb. FormBuilder has a method group which takes in a shortened code for new FormControl as compared to:

```
form = new FormGroup({
    username: new FormControl ('', Validators.required),
    password: new FormControl ('', Validators.required)
});
```

Essentially, FormBuilder is syntactic sugar that shortens the new FormGroup(), new FormControl() code that can build up in larger forms. This results in cleaner and more compact for large forms.

```
    this.form = fb.group({
        username:['',Validators.required],
        password:['',Validators.required]
    })
```

Like new FormControl, the first element is the default value and the second element is the validator function. Note that both are optional and it is not mandatory to specify them.

Finally, the group method returns a FormGroup object as a result and we store it in *form*.

7.4 Implementing Custom Validation

While there are a couple of built-in validators provided by Angular like *required, min/maxlength*, we often need to add some custom validation capabilities to our application's form to fulfill our needs for example, a valid password cannot contain a space. In this section, we will implement a custom validator that checks if a password has space in it.

First, in *app*, add a new file passwordValidator.ts. This class will include all validation rules for the password field. Fill it in with the below codes.

```
import { FormControl } from '@angular/forms';

export class PasswordValidator{
  static cannotContainSpace(formControl: FormControl){
    if(formControl.value.indexOf(' ') >= 0)
      return { cannotContainSpace: true };

    return null;
  }
}
```

Code Explanation

We declare a static method *cannotContainSpace* that takes in a FormControl object as argument. We access the value string property of the formControl and check if there are spaces in it with the *indexOf* method. If there are, we return { cannotContainSpace: true }, and if there are not spaces, we return *null*.

Note that Angular validators work this way; If the validation passes, return null. If it fails, return {<validationRule>:<value>} where <value> can be anything. It can be a boolean true/false, or an object that supplies more data about the validation error.

login.component.ts

Next, we apply the *cannotContainSpace* validator to the *password* field. Back in login.component.ts, add the lines in **bold**.

```
import { Component } from '@angular/core';
import { FormBuilder, FormGroup, Validators } from '@angular/forms';

import { PasswordValidator } from './passwordValidator';

@Component({
    selector:'login',
    templateUrl: 'login.component.html'
})
export class LoginComponent  {

    form: FormGroup;

    constructor(fb: FormBuilder){
        this.form = fb.group({
            username:['',Validators.required],
            password:['',Validators.compose([Validators.required,
                PasswordValidator.cannotContainSpace])]
```

74

```
        })
    }

    login(){
        console.log(this.form.value);
    }
}
```

Code Explanation

First, we import our PasswordValidator, and apply it to *password*. Because we have more than one validator on *password* form control, we need to compose the multiple validators by calling *Validators compose* method. The compose method takes in an array of Validators
[Validators.required, PasswordValidator.cannotContainSpace]

login.component.html

Finally, we implement the custom validation message placeholder. Back in login.component.html, replace the validation codes for *password* as shown in **bold** below.

```
<form [formGroup]="form" (ngSubmit)="login()">
    <div class="form-group">
        <label for="username">Username</label>
        <input type="text" class="form-control" formControlName="username">
        <div                              *ngIf="form.controls.username.touched
            && !form.controls.username.valid" class="alert alert-danger">
            Username is required
        </div>
    </div>
    <div class="form-group">
        <label for="password">Password</label>
        <input type="password" class="form-control" formControlName="password">
        <div *ngIf="form.controls.password.touched
            && form.controls.password.errors">
            <div *ngIf="form.controls.password.errors.required"
                    class="alert alert-danger">
              Password is required.
             </div>
            <div *ngIf="form.controls.password.errors.cannotContainSpace"
                    class="alert alert-danger">
                Password cannot contain space.
            </div>
        </div>
    </div>
    <button class="btn btn-primary" type="submit">Login</button>
</form>
```

Notice that we instead of checking for *!password.valid*, we now check for *password.errors*. This is because

75

there are now more than one kinds of error for *password* namely, *required* and *cannotContainSpace*, so we need to further have a nested **ngIf* for each error to check for each kind of error specifically.

When you run your app now and try to enter a password with space in it, you will get a validation error message like in figure 7.4.1.

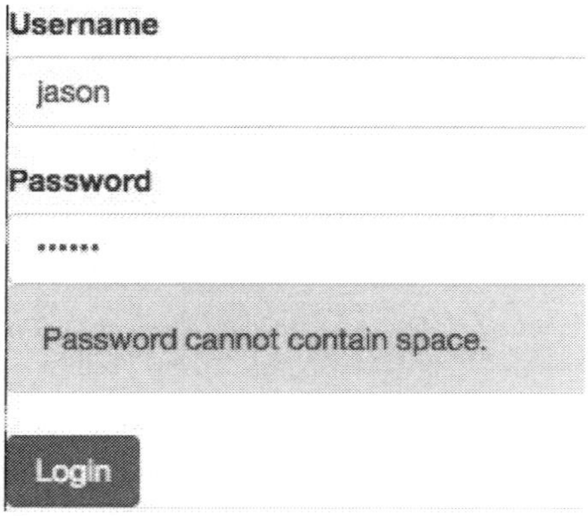

figure 7.4.1

7.5 Validating Upon Form Submit

There are times when you have to do validation upon submitting the form to the server. For example, validating username and password against the application's database. In the below example, we will illustrate validation of username and password upon submitting the login form.

First in *app* folder, create a new file login.service.ts which is the service class for login functionality. Remember that we should implement logic in service classes to keep our component classes lightweight and mainly for rendering displays. Fill in login.service.ts with the below code.

```
import {Injectable} from '@angular/core';

@Injectable()
export class LoginService {
  login(username, password){
    if(username === "jason" && password === "123")
        return true;
    else
        return false;
  }
}
```

Our login service class is a simple class with a method *login* that takes in argument *username* and *password*

76

credentials. We mark our Login service class as available for dependency injection by decorating it with the @Injectable() annotation.

In a real application, our *login* method should call an authentication api on a server with the credentials. To simplify our illustration for now, we authenticate with hardcoded values.

Do note that whenever we create a new service class and want to use it, we should specify it in the *providers* array of our module class to state that we want to use this service in that module. In our case, since we have only one module AppModule, we specify it in *providers: [LoginService]* of app.module.ts. We will cover more about modules and their providers in **Chapter 11 - Structuring Large Apps With Modules**.

Next in login.component.ts, add the below codes in **bold**.

```
import { Component } from '@angular/core';
import { FormBuilder, FormGroup, Validators } from '@angular/forms';

import { PasswordValidator } from './passwordValidator';
import { LoginService } from './login.service';

@Component({
    selector:'login',
    templateUrl: 'login.component.html'
})
export class LoginComponent   {

    form: FormGroup;

    constructor(fb: FormBuilder, private _loginService: LoginService){

        this.form = fb.group({
            username:['',Validators.required ],
             password:['',Validators.compose([Validators.required,
                                PasswordValidator.cannotContainSpace])]
        })
    }

    login(){
      var result = this._loginService.login(this.form.controls['username'].value,
                                  this.form.controls['password'].value);

        if(!result){
            this.form.controls['password'].setErrors({
                invalidLogin: true
            });
        }
    }
}
```

Code Explanation

We import and use dependency injection in the constructor to get an instance of LoginService. We then have a method *login()* that calls the *login* method in our *loginService* instance with the user-keyed in values of *username* and *password*.

```
this.form.controls['username'].value
this.form.controls['password'].value
```

With the above code, we access the *value* property of *username* and *password* control inside *form* to get the user keyed-in values.

```
if(!result){
    this.form.controls['password'].setErrors({
        invalidLogin: true
    });
}
```

The login method returns *result* as *true* if the login credentials are valid. If *false*, we access the *password* FormControl with *this.form.controls['password']* and call its *setErrors* method to supply the error *invalidLogin: true*. As mentioned earlier, *true* can also be replaced with a value or object to provide more details about the validation.

login.component.html

Lastly, we add a *div* to login.component.html for our login validation message.

In login.component.html, add the below codes in **bold**.

```
<div class="form-group">
    <label for="password">Password</label>
    <input type="password" class="form-control" formControlName="password">
    <div *ngIf="form.controls.password.touched && form.controls.password.errors">
        <div *ngIf="form.controls.password.errors.invalidLogin"
            class="alert alert-danger">
            Username or password is invalid.
        </div>
        <div *ngIf="form.controls.password.errors.required"
            class="alert alert-danger">
            Password is required.
        </div>
        <div *ngIf="form.controls.password.errors.cannotContainSpace"
            class="alert alert-danger">
            Password cannot contain space.
        </div>
    </div>
</div>
```

We use a *ngIf* to check for the error *invalidLogin* and display the alert message "Username or password is invalid". Run your app now and if you do not supply a valid *username* and *password*, you should get the invalid login message as shown in figure 7.5.1.

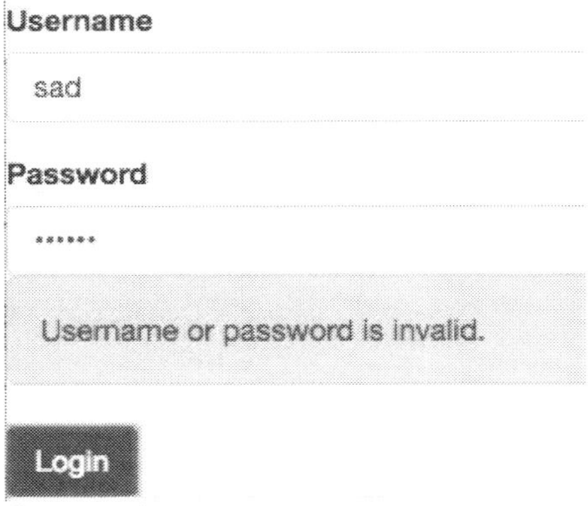

Username

sad

Password

••••••

Username or password is invalid.

Login

figure 7.5.1

Summary

In this chapter, we learnt how to implement model driven forms in Angular. We learnt how to create FormControl and FormGroup objects, use FormBuilder to make our code more compact, how to implement custom validation, and how to validate the form upon submit. Now after submitting a form, we need to persist the data by calling the api endpoint of the server. We will begin to explore on how to communicate with the server in the next few chapters.

CHAPTER 8: INTRODUCTION TO OBSERVABLES

For Angular to connect to backend servers, we need Observables which is a concept introduced in a library called Reactive Extensions. Reactive Extensions is a comprehensive library by itself independent from Angular. If you wish to know more about it, you can go to *reactivex.io*. The *rxjs* folder in *node_modules* contains the Reactive Extensions library for Javascript used by Angular.

In Reactive Extensions, an observer (or sometimes called subscriber or watcher) subscribes to an Observable. That observer reacts to whatever item or sequence of items the Observable emits. This asynchronous pattern facilitates concurrent operations because it does not need to block while waiting for the Observable to emit objects, but instead it creates an observer that stands ready to respond appropriately at whatever future time the Observable emits.

Later on, we will be implementing a search GitHub results app using Observables where the user enters her search key words and a request is sent to the GitHub server. The inputing of search key words, the request for GitHub search results and rendering of the search results may execute in parallel because of Observables thereby resulting in a smooth experience for the user.

8.1 Observables

An Observable represents an asynchronous data stream where data arrives asynchronously. An example is the *keyup* event from a textbox. User input arrives asynchronously and we can model it as an Observable stream.

For an Observable stream, we subscribe to it and give it a **callback function**.

```
function(newData){
  ...
}
```

When a new data element arrives, it will push that data element to us by calling the provided function back. We thus call the provided function a **callback function**.

Because we observe Observable streams and get notified when data arrives asynchronously, we call them Observables.

8.2 Creating an observable from DOM events

We will illustrate Observables by creating an Observable stream from the keyup event of a textbox. Suppose we want to implement a search service to look up users' data on *GitHub.com*. We do this by typing a search term into the input box and then call the GitHub api to get user data with a similar name.

First, either re-use the project you have from previous chapters or create a new project using Angular CLI. Make sure that you import *ReactiveFormsModule* in app.module.ts. Then, copy the following code into app component.

```
import { Component } from '@angular/core';
import { FormControl } from '@angular/forms';

@Component({
  selector: 'app-root',
  template: `
    <input class="form-control" type="search"
      [formControl]="searchControl">
  `
})
export class AppComponent {
  searchControl = new FormControl();

  constructor(){
    this.searchControl.valueChanges.subscribe(value => {
      console.log(value);
    });
  }
}
```

Code Explanation

```
    <input class="form-control" type="search"
      [formControl]="searchControl">
```

Because our search input consists of just one input control, we do not need a <form> element for it. We can use the *formControl* directive in the input control. The *formControl* represents our input field.

The *formControl* class has a property *valueChanges* (see below) which returns an Observable. We can subscribe to this observable by calling the *subscribe* method. In this way, we get notified whenever the value in the input field changes.

```
  constructor() {
    this.searchControl.valueChanges.subscribe(value => {
      console.log(value);
    });
  }
```

The *subscribe* method requires a function as argument. This function will be called by the Observable when new data arrives (i.e. value in input field changes). You can declare a function using the traditional anonymous function syntax like

```
function (value){
  console.log(value);
}
```

or you can shorten this code and use the arrow function (or lambda expression syntax).

```
value => {
      console.log(value);
}
```

Every time we press a key in the textbox, we get the text value pushed to us in an Observable stream. Our callback function gets called and we print the value to the console (fig. 7.2.1).

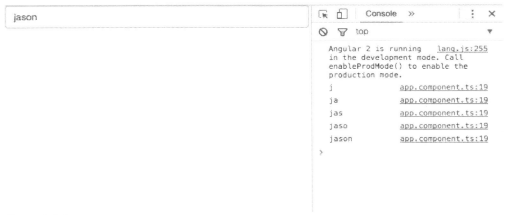

figure 8.2.1

8.3 Observable Operators

So what is the benefit of Observables? The benefit of Observables is that it provides a set of operators that we can use to transform, filter, aggregate and combine data received from the observable stream. In the following, we look at some of the operators:

filter Operator

In our input, say we want to call GitHub only if the user types at least three characters so as not to flood GitHub with too many requests. To do so, we can apply the *filter* operator. We do so by first importing the *filter* operator with the below code

83

```
import { filter } from 'rxjs/operators';
```

and add the filter operator as shown below in **bold**.

```
this.searchControl.valueChanges
  .pipe(filter(text => text.length >= 3))
  .subscribe(value => {
    console.log(value);
});
```

The *filter* operator takes an expression *text.length >= 3* and determines that the value should be selected only if the expression returns true. We wrap the *filter* operator function call with the *pipe()* method. When we have more than one operator (which we will demonstrate later), the *pipe* method executes them from left to right.

debounceTime Operator

Suppose we want to wait 400 milliseconds in between requests before calling GitHub, we can apply the *debounceTime* operator. We do so by first importing the *debounceTime* operator with the below code

```
import { filter,debounceTime } from 'rxjs/operators';
```

Next, we add the *debounceTime* operator as shown below.

```
this.searchControl.valueChanges
  .pipe(filter(text => text.length >= 3), debounceTime(400))
  .subscribe(value => {
    console.log(value);
});
```

The *pipe* method now contains the *filter* operator and the *debounceTime* operator. *pipe()* executes them from left to right meaning it executes *filter* first followed by *debounceTime*. Thus, you can see that the benefit of Observable operators is that you can keep applying operators for the custom logic that you want.

distinctUntilChanged Operator

Say if a user presses the left and right arrow keys to move the cursor, the *valueChange* event is fired and we send multiple requests with the same input string to GitHub since the text in the input field is not changed. To avoid such multiple requests with the same search term, we can apply the *distinctUntilChanged* operator which will let us receive our Observable only when the text is changed. We do so by first importing the *distinctUntilChanged* operator with the below code

```
import { filter,debounceTime,distinctUntilChanged } from 'rxjs/operators';
```

Next, add the *distinctUntilChanged* operator as shown below.

```
this.searchControl.valueChanges
  .pipe(filter(text => text.length >= 3), debounceTime(400),distinctUntilChanged())
  .subscribe(value => {
    console.log(value);
  });
```

Final Code

Below shows the final code for our app component.

```
import { Component } from '@angular/core';
import { FormControl } from '@angular/forms';
import { filter,debounceTime,distinctUntilChanged } from 'rxjs/operators';

@Component({
  selector: 'app-root',
  template: `
    <input class="form-control" type="search"
[formControl]="searchControl">
  `
})
export class AppComponent {
  searchControl = new FormControl();

  constructor(){
    this.searchControl.valueChanges
      .pipe(filter(text => text.length >= 3),
            debounceTime(400),distinctUntilChanged())
      .subscribe(value => {
        console.log(value);
      });
  }
}
```

Summary

In this chapter, we are introduced to Observables, how to subscribe to Observables from DOM events, and how to apply certain Observable operators like *filter*, *debounceTime* and *distinctUntilChanged* to avoid sending multiple repeated requests.

Now that we can get an Observable stream from an input, we will learn how to use the search terms keyed into the input to get data from a server in the next chapter.

Chapter 9: Getting Data From RESTful APIs with Observables

With the knowledge of how to subscribe to Observables, we will see how to call backend services to get data through RESTful APIs in this chapter.

9.1 GitHub RESTful API

Building RESTful APIs is beyond the scope of Angular because Angular is a client side technology whereas building RESTful APIs require server side technology like NodeJS, ASP.NET, Ruby on Rails and so on. (But later on in chapter 12, we will introduce Firebase, which provides us with a simple way for us to create and store server-side data that we can utilize to build a fully functioning Angular application!)

We will illustrate by connecting to the GitHub RESTful API to retrieve and manage GitHub content. You can know more about the GitHub API at

```
https://developer.github.com/v3/
```

But as a quick introduction, we can get GitHub users data with the following url,

```
https://api.github.com/search/users?q=<search term>
```

We simply specify our search term in the url to get GitHub data for user with name matching our search term. An example is shown below with search term *greg*.

```
https://api.github.com/search/users?q=greg
```

When we make a call to this url, we will get the following json objects as a result (fig. 9.1.1).

```
                     C  ⌂    🔒 Secure   https://api.github.com/search/users?q=greg
```

```
{
  "total_count": 14813,
  "incomplete_results": false,
  "items": [
    {
      "login": "gregkh",
      "id": 14953,
      "avatar_url": "https://avatars0.githubusercontent.com/u/14953?v=3",
      "gravatar_id": "",
      "url": "https://api.github.com/users/gregkh",
      "html_url": "https://github.com/gregkh",
      "followers_url": "https://api.github.com/users/gregkh/followers",
      "following_url": "https://api.github.com/users/gregkh/following{/other_user}",
      "gists_url": "https://api.github.com/users/gregkh/gists{/gist_id}",
      "starred_url": "https://api.github.com/users/gregkh/starred{/owner}{/repo}",
      "subscriptions_url": "https://api.github.com/users/gregkh/subscriptions",
      "organizations_url": "https://api.github.com/users/gregkh/orgs",
      "repos_url": "https://api.github.com/users/gregkh/repos",
      "events_url": "https://api.github.com/users/gregkh/events{/privacy}",
      "received_events_url": "https://api.github.com/users/gregkh/received_events",
      "type": "User",
      "site_admin": false,
      "score": 45.86066
    },
    {
      "login": "greg",
      "id": 1658846,
      "avatar_url": "https://avatars0.githubusercontent.com/u/1658846?v=3",
      "gravatar_id": "",
      "url": "https://api.github.com/users/greg",
      "html_url": "https://github.com/greg",
      "followers_url": "https://api.github.com/users/greg/followers",
      "following_url": "https://api.github.com/users/greg/following{/other_user}",
      "gists_url": "https://api.github.com/users/greg/gists{/gist_id}",
      "starred_url": "https://api.github.com/users/greg/starred{/owner}{/repo}",
      "subscriptions_url": "https://api.github.com/users/greg/subscriptions",
      "organizations_url": "https://api.github.com/users/greg/orgs",
      "repos_url": "https://api.github.com/users/greg/repos",
      "events_url": "https://api.github.com/users/greg/events{/privacy}",
      "received_events_url": "https://api.github.com/users/greg/received_events",
      "type": "User",
      "site_admin": false,
      "score": 44.028103
    },
```

fig. 9.1.1

9.2 Getting Data

To get data using a RESTful API, we are going to use the *HttpClient* class in Angular. We use it to make requests to the server. The *HttpClient* class provides the *get()* method for getting a resource, *post()* for creating it, *put()* for updating it and *delete()* for deleting a resource.

We will first create a service which will be responsible for talking to our RESTful API. Our components should not make http calls directly but rather delegate that role to services.

Create a new Angular project (remember to add the bootstrap link in index.html) and in the *app* folder, create a new file *github.service.ts* with the below code.

```
import {HttpClient} from '@angular/common/http';
import {Observable} from 'rxjs';

export interface GitHubUser{
    html_url: string;
    avatar_url: string;
    login: string;
    score: string;
}

export class GitHubService{
    constructor(private _http: HttpClient){

    }

    getGitHubData(_searchTerm):Observable<GitHubUser>{
      return this._http.get<GitHubUser>
        ("https://api.github.com/search/users?q="+_searchTerm);
    }
}
```

Code Explanation

getGitHubData is a method that will return GitHub data from our api end point. To call our api end point, we need to use the *HttpClient* service of Angular. We import it using:

```
import {HttpClient} from '@angular/common/http';
```

We then declare the GitHubUser interface. We use this interface to describe the expected type of the response returned from GitHub. We will only be extracting the *html_url*, *avatar_url*, *login* and *score* fields.

```
export interface GitHubUser{
    html_url: string;
    avatar_url: string;
    login: string;
    score: string;
}
```

We inject the *HttpClient* class into the constructor of our GitHub Service. Remember dependency injection? We let Angular create an instance of *HttpClient* class and give it to us. Our constructor has a

89

parameter *_http* which is of type *HttpClient*. By convention, we prefix private fields with an underscore '_'.

```
constructor(private _http: HttpClient){

}
```

In *getGitHubData*, we use the *get()* method of *HttpClient* and give the url of our api endpoint. We have a search term provided by the user from an input which we will implement later. The return type of *get()* is an Observable of <GitHubUser>. By specifying <GitHubUser> type, we indicate the type of the response wrapped inside the Observable. So we will return this Observable in our service and our component will be the consumer of this Observable. We will subscribe to it and when an ajax call is completed, the response is fed to the Observable and then pushed to the component.

```
getGitHubData(_searchTerm):Observable<GitHubUser>{
  return this._http.get<GitHubUser>
    ("https://api.github.com/search/users?q="+_searchTerm);
}
```

HttpClientModule

Because we are using *HttpClient*, we need to import *HttpClientModule* in our AppModule class. Add the codes below in bold to app.module.ts:

app.module.ts

```
import { BrowserModule } from '@angular/platform-browser';
import { NgModule } from '@angular/core';

import { AppComponent } from './app.component';
import { HttpClientModule } from '@angular/common/http';

@NgModule({
  declarations: [
    AppComponent
  ],
  imports: [
    BrowserModule,
    HttpClientModule
  ],
  providers: [],
  bootstrap: [AppComponent]
})
```

```
export class AppModule {  }
```

9.3 Dependency Injection

Next, we inject our service into our component. As covered in chapter 7, we do so by first marking our GitHub service class as available for dependency injection. We decorate it with the *@Injectable()* annotation as shown below.

```
import {HttpClient} from '@angular/common/http';
import {Observable} from 'rxjs';
import {Injectable} from '@angular/core';

export interface GitHubUser{
    html_url: string;
    avatar_url: string;
    login: string;
    score: string;
}

@Injectable()
export class GitHubService{
    constructor(private _http: HttpClient){

    }

    getGitHubData(_searchTerm):Observable<GitHubUser>{
      return this._http.get<GitHubUser>
        ("https://api.github.com/search/users?q="+_searchTerm);
    }
}
```

Code Explanation

After importing the Injectable annotation.

```
import { Injectable } from '@angular/core';
```

We then apply it to the top of the class

```
@Injectable()
export class GitHubService{
```

and the service is now ready for injection. Now let's go to app.component.ts.

91

app.component.ts

```
import { Component } from '@angular/core';
import { GitHubService } from './github.service';

@Component({
  selector: 'app-root',
  template: `
  `,
  providers: [GitHubService]
})
export class AppComponent {

  constructor(private _githubService: GitHubService){
    this._githubService.getGitHubData('greg')
      .subscribe(data => console.log(data));
  }

}
```

Code Explanation

First, we import the service.

```
import { GitHubService } from './github.service';
```

We then inject it into the constructor.

```
  constructor(private _githubService: GitHubService){
    this._githubService.getGitHubData('greg')
      .subscribe(data => console.log(data));
  }
```

Remember that in dependency injection, Angular looks at the constructor and sees a parameter of type GitHubService and seeks to create an instance of it. To let the injector know where to find the GitHubService to create it, we register the GitHubService by specifying it in the *providers* property in the component's metadata.

```
@Component({
  selector: 'app-root',
  template: `
  `,
  providers: [GitHubService]
```

92

})

Now that we are done with the dependency injection, let's use our service. In the constructor, we call the *getGitHubData* method with argument 'greg' from our _*githubService* instance. The *getGitHubData* method returns an Observable which we need to subscribe to.

```
constructor(private _githubService: GitHubService){
  this._githubService.getGitHubData('greg')
    .subscribe(data => console.log(data));
}
```

We then pass in our callback function *data => console.log(data)*.

When we run our app in the browser, we get the following result from the server (fig. 9.3.1).

```
▼ {total_count: 18198, incomplete_results: false, items: Array(30)}
    incomplete_results: false
  ▼ items: Array(30)
    ▶ 0: {login: "greg", id: 1658846, avatar_url: "https://avatars3.gith
    ▶ 1: {login: "gdb", id: 211857, avatar_url: "https://avatars3.github
    ▶ 2: {login: "gregkh", id: 14953, avatar_url: "https://avatars3.gith
    ▶ 3: {login: "wincent", id: 7074, avatar_url: "https://avatars0.gith
    ▶ 4: {login: "gregheo", id: 77462, avatar_url: "https://avatars0.git
    ▶ 5: {login: "myfreeweb", id: 208340, avatar_url: "https://avatars0.
    ▶ 6: {login: "pixelass", id: 1148334, avatar_url: "https://avatars3.
    ▶ 7: {login: "gmaxwell", id: 858454, avatar_url: "https://avatars1.g
    ▶ 8: {login: "gregmalcolm", id: 64433, avatar_url: "https://avatars3
    ▶ 9: {login: "sellout", id: 33031, avatar_url: "https://avatars2.git
    ▶ 10: {login: "gregwebs", id: 1183, avatar_url: "https://avatars2.gi
    ▶ 11: {login: "gregrickaby", id: 200280, avatar_url: "https://avatar
    ▶ 12: {login: "gshackles", id: 196182, avatar_url: "https://avatars0
```

figure 9.3.1

We are returned a single object containing an items array of size 30 each representing the data of a GitHub user.

Each *user* object has properties *avatar_url*, *html_url*, *login*, *score*, and so on (fig. 9.3.2).

```
▼ items: Array(30)
  ▼ 0:
      avatar_url: "https://avatars3.githubusercontent.com/u/1658846?v=4"
      events_url: "https://api.github.com/users/greg/events{/privacy}"
      followers_url: "https://api.github.com/users/greg/followers"
      following_url: "https://api.github.com/users/greg/following{/other_user}"
      gists_url: "https://api.github.com/users/greg/gists{/gist_id}"
      gravatar_id: ""
      html_url: "https://github.com/greg"
      id: 1658846
      login: "greg"
      organizations_url: "https://api.github.com/users/greg/orgs"
      received_events_url: "https://api.github.com/users/greg/received_events"
      repos_url: "https://api.github.com/users/greg/repos"
      score: 52.85922
      site_admin: false
      starred_url: "https://api.github.com/users/greg/starred{/owner}{/repo}"
      subscriptions_url: "https://api.github.com/users/greg/subscriptions"
      type: "User"
      url: "https://api.github.com/users/greg"
```

figure 9.3.2

To get the *items* array direct, (since that is the data we want), we can further specify it like below

```
this._githubService.getGitHubData('greg')
      .subscribe(data => console.log(data.items));
```

Doing so will get us the items array objects straight like in figure 9.3.3

```
                                                    app.component.ts:6
(30) [Object, Object, Object, Object, Object, Object, Object, Object, Object,
 Object, Object, Object, Object, Object, Object, Object, Object, Object, Object,
 Object, Object, Object, Object, Object, Object, Object, Object, Object, Object,
 Object]
  ▶ 0: Object
  ▶ 1: Object
  ▶ 2: Object
  ▶ 3: Object
  ▶ 4: Object
  ▶ 5: Object
  ▶ 6: Object
  ▶ 7: Object
  ▶ 8: Object
  ▶ 9: Object
  ▶ 10: Object
  ▶ 11: Object
  ▶ 12: Object
  ▶ 13: Object
  ▶ 14: Object
  ▶ 15: Object
  ▶ 16: Object
  ▶ 17: Object
  ▶ 18: Object
  ▶ 19: Object
  ▶ 20: Object
  ▶ 21: Object
  ▶ 22: Object
```

figure 9.3.3

9.4 ngOnInit

Even though our code currently works, it doesn't follow best practises. We are currently calling the server in the constructor of the app component. As a best practise, constructors should be lightweight and should not contain any costly operations making it easier to test and debug. So where should we move our code to?

Components have a lifecycle which is managed by Angular. There are lifecycle hooks which we can tap into during key moments in the component's lifecycle. To do this, we need to implement one or more of the following interfaces in the component.

OnInit
OnDestroy
DoCheck
OnChanges
AfterContentInit
AfterContentChecked
AfterViewInit
AfterViewChecked

Each of the interfaces has a method that we can implement in our component. When the right moment arrives, Angular will call these methods. For example, we can implement the *OnInit* interface to be notified when a component is first instantiated.

By convention, the name of the method is the same name as the interface with the prefix *ng*. E.g. *ngOnInit*.

We will implement the *ngOnInit()* method. This method will be called when Angular instantiates our component. In terms of lifecycle, it is called after the constructor. So in the constructor, we do lightweight and basic initialization and if we need to call the server, we do it in *ngOnInit*. So we shift the code to call GitHub from the constructor to *ngOnInit* as shown below.

```
export class AppComponent {

  constructor(private _githubService: GitHubService){
  }

  ngOnInit() {
    this._githubService.getGitHubData('greg')
      .subscribe(data => console.log(data.items));
  }
}
```

9.5 Showing a Loader Icon

When getting content from a server, it is often useful to show a loading icon to the user. To do so, in app component, create a variable called *isLoading* and set it to *true* like in the below code.

```
export class AppComponent {
  isLoading = true;
  ...
```

Next, in the *subscribe* method, set *isLoading* to false because at this point, we get the results from the server and loading is finished.

```
  ngOnInit() {
    this._githubService.getGitHubData('greg')
      .subscribe(data => {
        this.isLoading = false;
        console.log(data.items)
      });
  }
```

Lastly, in the template, add a *div* that shows the loading icon. We use **ngIf* to make the *div* visible only when the component is loading.

```
template: `
  <div *ngIf="isLoading">Getting data...</div>
`,
```

If you load your app in the browser, you should see the "Getting data" message being displayed for a short moment before data from the server is loaded.

We will now replace the "Getting data" message with the loading icon. To get the loading icon, *google* 'font awesome' and the first result should be http://fontawesome.io/. Font awesome is a library similar to glyphicons that gives us many useful icons. Go to 'Get Started' and follow the instructions to copy the embed code and paste it into the head section of index.html.

Back in app component, replace the message with the icon like in the below code.

```
template: `
        <div *ngIf="isLoading">
          <i class="fa fa-spinner fa-spin fa-3x"></i>
        </div>
`,
```

To add a *font awesome* icon, we use the *<i>* tag. fa is the base class for all font awesome icons. *fa-spinner* renders the spinner icon. *fa-spin* adds the animation to it. *fa-3x* makes the icon three times bigger so that it is easier to see.

9.6 Implementing a GitHub Results Display Page

We will now implement a page which displays our GitHub user data nicely like in figure 9.6.1. To do so, we use the Bootstrap Media Object component (https://getbootstrap.com/docs/4.1/layout/media-object/ *version 4.1 as of time writing*) as what we have done previously. We will be copying the markup from getbootstrap, pasting it into our component and filling the missing parts with interpolation strings.

GitHub User Results

gregkh
Score: 45.635616

greg
Score: 44.03208

gdb
Score: 38.98523

gregheo
Score: 38.670673

figure 9.6.1

Firstly, note that the images that we get from GitHub are of different height and width. To make all images of different height and width display the same in our page for e.g. 100px by 100px, we define the following inline css style class *img*.

app.component.ts

```
@Component({
  selector: 'app-root',
    styles: [`
      .img {
          position: relative;
          float: left;
          width:  100px;
          height: 100px;
          background-position: 50% 50%;
          background-repeat:   no-repeat;
          background-size:     cover;
      }
    `],
```

In the template, we will be copying the markup from *getbootstrap* and paste it into our component as shown below.

```
template: `
    <div *ngIf="isLoading">
      <i class="fa fa-spinner fa-spin fa-3x"></i>
    </div>
    <h3>GitHub User Results</h3>
    <div *ngIf="isLoading">
      <i class="fa fa-spinner fa-spin fa-3x"></i>
    </div>
    <div *ngFor="let user of users" class="media">
        <div class="media-left">
            <a href="{{ user.html_url }}">
            <img class="media-object img"
              src="{{ user.avatar_url }}" alt="...">
            </a>
        </div>
        <div class="media-body">
            <h4 class="media-heading">{{ user.login }}</h4>
            Score: {{ user.score }}
        </div>
    </div>
`,
```

Code Explanation

```
    <div *ngIf="isLoading">
      <i class="fa fa-spinner fa-spin fa-3x"></i>
    </div>
```

We have added the loading icon as implemented previously.

```
    <div *ngFor="let user of users" class="media">
```

We then apply *ngFor* to repeat the media object for each user we get from GitHub.

We then add four string interpolations inside the template. The user's html_url, avatar_url, login id and her score.

```
    <div *ngFor="let user of users" class="media">
        <div class="media-left">
```

99

```
            <a href="{{ user.html_url }}">
            <img class="media-object img"
              src="{{ user.avatar_url }}" alt="...">
            </a>
        </div>
        <div class="media-body">
            <h4 class="media-heading">{{ user.login }}</h4>
            Score: {{ user.score }}
        </div>
    </div>
</div>
```

In our *ngFor*, we state *let user of users*. But where do we get our *users* array instantiated and assigned with content?

We declare it in app component *users = []* as shown below (Add the below codes in **bold** into app.component.ts). We then subscribe to our Observable returned from our GitHub service and assign the returned result to *users* array. Note that we assign it with *data.items* as this is the users *item* array structured in the json response.

```
export class AppComponent {
  isLoading = true;

  users = [];

  constructor(private _githubService: GitHubService){

  }

 ngOnInit() {
    this._githubService.getGitHubData('greg')
      .subscribe(data => {
        this.isLoading = false;
        this.users = data.items;
        //console.log(data.items)
      });
  }

}
```

If you run your app now, you should get a similar page as shown below.

GitHub User Results

gregkh
Score: 45.635616

greg
Score: 44.03208

gdb
Score: 38.98523

gregheo
Score: 38.670673

9.7 Adding an Input to GitHub Results Display Page

We are currently hard-coding our search term to '*greg*' in our request to GitHub. We will now use the search input that we have implemented in chapter eight and combine it with our code here so that as a user types in her search terms, the result can be displayed.

In chapter eight, we subscribe to an Observable stream from our input in the constructor of app component as shown below.

```
constructor(){
  this.searchControl.valueChanges
    .pipe(filter(text => text.length >= 3),
          debounceTime(400),
          distinctUntilChanged())
    .subscribe(value => {
      console.log(value);
  });
}
```

As mentioned earlier, such code should instead be placed in *ngOnInit* since the constructor should be lightweight. Also, we will move the code to subscribe to our GitHub Service into the callback function code block of *valueChanges* (see below). Remember that we have to import the *filter*, *debounceTime*, *distinctUntilChanged* operators as well.

```
constructor(){
  this.searchControl.valueChanges
    .pipe(filter(text => text.length >= 3),
         debounceTime(400),
         distinctUntilChanged())
    .subscribe(value => {
      // insert call to GitHub service here
    });
}
```

The final app component code will look like below. Make sure that you add the import statements for the *filter*, *debounceTime*, *distinctUntilChanged* operators and *FormControl* for our input search field.

Note that we initialize *isLoading* to *false* at first since no call to GitHub is made at the beginning. Once we get a notification from *valueChanges* Observable, we then set *isLoading* to *true* just before the call to *getGitHubData* to show the loading icon. Once we get notified of results from our GitHub service Observable, we set *isLoading* to *false* to hide the loading icon.

app.component.ts

```
import { Component } from '@angular/core';
import { GitHubService } from './github.service';

import { filter,debounceTime,distinctUntilChanged } from
'rxjs/operators';
import { FormControl } from '@angular/forms';

@Component({
  selector: 'app-root',
  styles: [`
    .img {
        position: relative;
        float: left;
        width:  100px;
        height: 100px;
        background-position: 50% 50%;
        background-repeat:   no-repeat;
        background-size:     cover;
    }
  `],
  template: `
```

```
    <div *ngIf="isLoading">
      <i class="fa fa-spinner fa-spin fa-3x"></i>
    </div>
    <h3>GitHub User Results</h3>
    <div *ngFor="let user of users" class="media">
        <div class="media-left">
            <a href="{{ user.html_url }}">
            <img class="media-object img"
              src="{{ user.avatar_url }}" alt="...">
            </a>
        </div>
        <div class="media-body">
            <h4 class="media-heading">{{ user.login }}</h4>
            Score: {{ user.score }}
        </div>
    </div>
  `,
  providers: [GitHubService]
})
export class AppComponent {
  searchControl = new FormControl();
  isLoading = false;
  users = [];
  constructor(private _githubService: GitHubService){
  }

  ngOnInit() {
    this.searchControl.valueChanges
        .pipe(filter(text => text.length >= 3),
debounceTime(400),distinctUntilChanged())
        .subscribe(value => {
          this.isLoading = true;
          this._githubService.getGitHubData(value)
              .subscribe(data => {
                 this.isLoading = false;
                 this.users = data.items;
          });
    });
  }
}
```

Next, add the *<input>* tag to the template at the top:

```
template: `
    <input class="form-control" type="search"
        [formControl]="searchControl">
    <div *ngIf="isLoading">
```

103

```
        <i class="fa fa-spinner fa-spin fa-3x"></i>
    </div>
    <h3>GitHub User Results</h3>
    <div *ngIf="isLoading">
        <i class="fa fa-spinner fa-spin fa-3x"></i>
    </div>
    <div *ngFor="let user of users" class="media">
        <div class="media-left">
            <a href="{{ user.html_url }}">
            <img class="media-object img"
              src="{{ user.avatar_url }}" alt="...">
            </a>
        </div>
        <div class="media-body">
            <h4 class="media-heading">{{ user.login }}</h4>
            Score: {{ user.score }}
        </div>
    </div>
    `,
```

Lastly, remember that you have import *ReactiveFormsModule* in app.module.ts since we are using reactive forms here.

app.module.ts

```
import { BrowserModule } from '@angular/platform-browser';
import { NgModule } from '@angular/core';

import { AppComponent } from './app.component';
import { HttpClientModule } from '@angular/common/http';
import { ReactiveFormsModule } from '@angular/forms';

@NgModule({
  declarations: [
    AppComponent
  ],
  imports: [
    BrowserModule,
    HttpClientModule,
    ReactiveFormsModule
  ],
  providers: [],
  bootstrap: [AppComponent]
})
```

```
export class AppModule {  }
```

You can now see GitHub user results displayed as you key in your search terms. And remember, because of the operators that we have earlier applied to our Observable, we do not send unnecessary multiple requests to GitHub.

Summary

In the chapter, we learned how implement a GitHub User Search application by connecting our Angular apps to the server RESTful api using Observables, HttpClient, component lifecycle hooks and display loader icons.

CHAPTER 10: ROUTING

We have so far covered components, directives and services. But what if we have multiple views that a user needs to navigate from one to the next? In this chapter, we will explore **Routers** that provide screen navigation in our Single Page Application.

We are familiar with navigating websites. We enter a URL in the address bar and the browser navigates to a corresponding page. We click links on the page and the browser navigates to a new page. We click the browser's back and forward buttons and the browser navigates backward and forward through the history of pages we've seen.

The Angular Router borrows from this model. It interprets a browser URL as an instruction to navigate to a client-generated view and can also pass optional parameters along to the supporting view component to help it decide what specific content to present.

We can bind the router to links on a page and it will navigate to the appropriate application view when the user clicks a link. We can also navigate imperatively when the user clicks a button, selects from a drop box, or from other user generated events. And because the router logs activity in the browser's history journal, so the back and forward buttons work as well.

In this chapter, we will extend our project from chapter 9 to add routing to navigate between Home, GitHub, User Signup Form components.

10.1 Enabling Routing

The first step to building a Single Page application is to enable routing. We need to ensure that we have set the *<base href="/">* base url in our index.html. Angular will use this to compose relative urls. If you have created your Angular project using the Angular CLI, *<base href="/">* should have been added for you under the head element in index.html as show below:

```
<head>
  <meta charset="utf-8">
  <title>Angular2Firstapp</title>
  <base href="/">
```

The / means that our Angular app is currently in the application root. If your application has a lot of modules, your directory might look something like the below:

```
/users
  /app
```

```
  index.html
/posts
  /app
  index.html
/albums
  /app
  index.html
```

The base href for albums index.html will then be *<base href="/albums/">*.

10.2 Setting Up Our Routes

After enabling routing, we need to define our routes. We define our routes in a separate new file. In your project from chapter 9, add a new file app.routing.ts with the below code:

```
import { NgModule } from '@angular/core';
import { Routes, RouterModule } from '@angular/router';

import { HomeComponent } from './home.component';
import { NotFoundComponent } from './notfound.component';
import { GitHubComponent } from './github.component';

export const routing = RouterModule.forRoot([
  {path: '', component: HomeComponent},
  {path: 'GitHub', component: GitHubComponent},
  {path: '**', component: NotFoundComponent}
]);
```

Code Explanation

app.routing.ts contains our route definitions.

```
import { Routes, RouterModule } from '@angular/router';
```

We import *Routes* and *RouterModule* from Router library which provide the essential routing functionalities.

```
export const routing = RouterModule.forRoot([
  {path: '', component: HomeComponent},
  {path: 'GitHub', component: GitHubComponent},
  {path: '**', component: NotFoundComponent}
]);
```

RouterModule has a method *forRoot* which takes an array of *Route* definition objects. *forRoot* returns a *module* object and we assign it to variable *routing*. We need to export *routing* so that we can later import it in App Module. Note that *routing* is declared as a *const* which is a good practise so that no one will modify our routes making our application more reliable.

We then pass in our array of *Route* definition objects into the *forRoot* method. Each route definition associates a path to a component. Each route definition has at least two properties, *path*, which is the unique name we assign to our route, and component which specifies the associated component.

In our route definition, we have specified three components. HomeComponent, NotFoundComponent and GitHubComponent. We have not yet created HomeComponent and NotFoundComponent. So create the below components in *app* folder now.

home.component.ts

```
import { Component } from '@angular/core';

@Component({
    template: '<h1>Home</h1>'
})
export class HomeComponent  {
}
```

notfound.component.ts

```
import { Component } from '@angular/core';

@Component({
    template: `
      <h1>Not Found</h1>
      `
})
export class NotFoundComponent { }
```

You will realize that HomeComponent and NotFoundComponent are very basic components that simply displays a message. This is for the purpose of illustrating navigating to different views.

github.component.ts

GitHub Component will simply contain the code we implemented back in chapter nine in App component. So, duplicate app.component.ts, rename it to github.component.ts and change the classname to *GitHubComponent*.

app.routing.ts

Back in app.routing.ts, we import the components we will use in our route definitions as shown below in **bold**.

```
import { NgModule } from '@angular/core';
import { Routes, RouterModule } from '@angular/router';

import { HomeComponent } from './home.component';
import { NotFoundComponent } from './notfound.component';
import { GitHubComponent } from './github.component';

export const routing = RouterModule.forRoot([
  {path: '', component: HomeComponent},
  {path: 'GitHub', component: GitHubComponent},
  {path: '**', component: NotFoundComponent}
]);
```

Now, our route definition tells Angular that:

- if the path changes to '', Angular should create an instance of HomeComponent and render it in the DOM.
- if the path changes to *'GitHub'*, Angular should create an instance of GitHubComponent and render it in the DOM.
- if a user navigates to a route that we have not defined, the path '**' is a wildcard that catches all invalid routes and directs to NotFoundComponent.

Next, in app.module.ts, we have to import and add our new components HomeComponent, NotFoundComponent and GitHubComponent to *declarations* array to declare that they are part of AppModule. We have to also import *routing* into the *imports* array as *routing* is a module which AppModule is dependent on.

The below lines in bold illustrate this.

app.module.ts

```
import { BrowserModule } from '@angular/platform-browser';
import { NgModule } from '@angular/core';
import { FormsModule } from '@angular/forms';
import { HttpClientModule } from '@angular/common/http';

import { AppComponent } from './app.component';
import { ReactiveFormsModule } from '@angular/forms';

import { HomeComponent } from './home.component';
import { NotFoundComponent } from './notfound.component';
```

110

```
import { GitHubComponent } from './github.component';
import { routing } from './app.routing';

@NgModule({
  declarations: [
    AppComponent,
    HomeComponent,
    NotFoundComponent,
    GitHubComponent
  ],
  imports: [
    BrowserModule,
    FormsModule,
    HttpClientModule,
    ReactiveFormsModule,
    routing
  ],
  providers: [],
  bootstrap: [AppComponent]
})
export class AppModule { }
```

10.3 Router Outlet and Links

Router Outlet

To specify where we want Angular to render our requested component when the user clicks on a link, we specify *<router-outlet></router-outlet>* in the DOM. For example in app.component.ts, we add *router-outlet* to the template:

```
import { Component } from '@angular/core';

@Component({
  selector: 'app-root',
  template: `
    <router-outlet></router-outlet>
    `,
  providers: []

})
export class AppComponent {
```

```
    constructor(){
    }
}
```

Router Links

Having defined and configured our routes in app.routing.ts, we can now add our navigation links to Home and GitHub component. In app.component.ts, add the below codes in bold.

```
import { Component } from '@angular/core';

@Component({
  selector: 'app-root',
  template: `
    <ul>
      <li><a routerLink="">Home</a></li>
      <li><a routerLink="GitHub">GitHub</a></li>
    </ul>
    <router-outlet></router-outlet>
    `
})
export class AppComponent {
}
```

Code Explanation

```
        <li><a routerLink="">Home</a></li>
        <li><a routerLink="GitHub">GitHub</a></li>
```

Note that we use *routerLink* directive instead of *href* to declare path to our routes. If we implement links using the traditional *href* way like below,

```
<li><a href="#">Home</a></li>
<li><a href="#">GitHub</a></li>
```

the `href` attribute will cause a full page reload which is contrary to the idea of Single Page Applications. In an SPA, we want our application to be loaded only once, and as we click on different links, only a part of the page is refreshed with the content of the target page. This results in much faster loading of pages.

We thus replace *href* with the *routerLink* directive and supply the name of the target route.

```
        <li><a routerLink="">Home</a></li>
        <li><a routerLink="GitHub">GitHub</a></li>
```

routerLink tells our *routing* component to navigate the user to the target route specified. The *routing* component finds the route definition with that name. It will then create an instance of the component and render it in the *router-outlet* element.

And if we try a non-existent route, we get a 'not found' page because we have earlier declared the wildcard path to direct to NotFoundComponent.

```
const routes: Routes = [
  {path: '', component: HomeComponent},
  {path: 'GitHub', component: GitHubComponent},
  {path: '**', component: NotFoundComponent}
];
```

If we run our app now, we'll get a view like in figure 10.3.1.

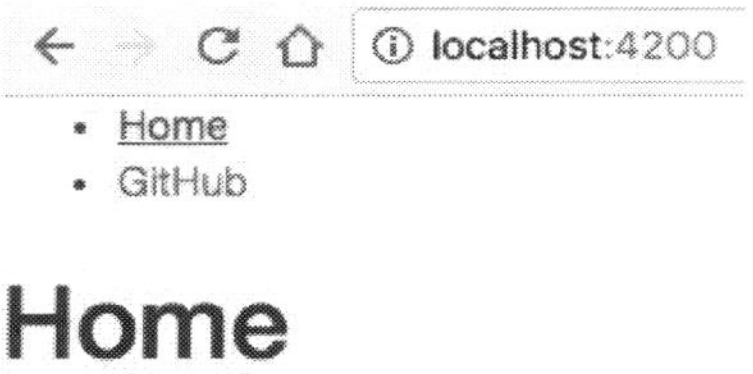

Home

figure 10.3.1

And if we navigate to GitHub, we get the view like in figure 10.3.2

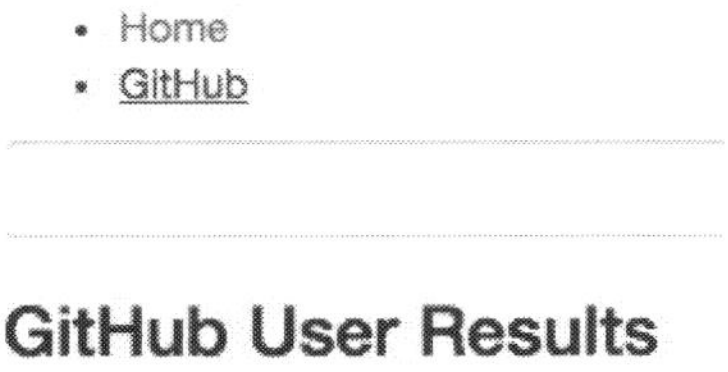

- Home
- GitHub

GitHub User Results

figure 10.3.2

Improving the Look of our Navbar Component

Our navbar currently does not look very professional. We will use the `navbar` component from **getbootstrap** (https://getbootstrap.com/docs/4.0/components/navbar/) to beautify our navigation bar. (As of time of writing this book, we are using bootstrap 4.0.0) Use the default *navbar* markup in the template of navbar component. The default navbar renders a complex navbar with many complex items like a form. Get rid of all the unnecessary stuff (like dropdown and search) and keep only the Home and GitHub links.

Below shows the code for app.component.ts with the navbar component markup in template copied from getbootstrap. Unnecessary *navbar* elements like *dropdown* and *search* have been removed to result in a cleaner code. You can see the code for the router links in **bold**.

app.component.ts

```
import { Component } from '@angular/core';

@Component({
  selector: 'app-root',
  template: `
    <nav class="navbar navbar-expand-lg navbar-light bg-light">
    <a class="navbar-brand" href="#">Navbar</a>
    <div class="collapse navbar-collapse" id="navbarSupportedContent">
      <ul class="navbar-nav mr-auto">
        <li class="nav-item active">
          <a class="nav-link" routerLink="">
            Home<span class="sr-only">(current)</span>
          </a>
        </li>
        <li class="nav-item">
          <a class="nav-link" routerLink="GitHub">GitHub</a>
        </li>
      </ul>
    </div>
    </nav>
    <router-outlet></router-outlet>
    `
})
export class AppComponent {
}
```

When you run your app now, you should get a more professional navigation bar like in figure 10.3.3.

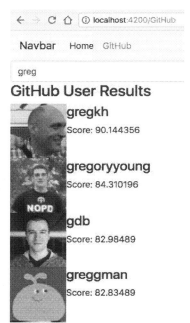

figure 10.3.3

And when you try to enter in an unspecified url, you get the NotFoundComponent rendered like in figure 10.3.4

Not Found

figure 10.3.4

Try it Yourself - Adding a new Router Link

Now, try adding a new router link on your own. Remember that you will have to add the new routerLink in App Component template like below:

```
<ul class="nav navbar-nav">
  <li><a routerLink="" routerLinkActive="active">Home</a></li>
  <li><a routerLink="GitHub" routerLinkActive="active">GitHub</a></li>
  <li><a routerLink="<path_name>" routerLinkActive="active">Path Text</a></li>
</ul>
```

Next in app.routing.ts, import the additional component and add the new path to the array in

RouterModule.forRoot as shown below:

```
import { HomeComponent } from './home.component';
...
import { YourOwnComponent } from './user-form.component';

export const routing = RouterModule.forRoot([
  {path: '', component: HomeComponent},
  {path: 'GitHub', component: GitHubComponent},
  {path: '<path_name>', component: YourOwnComponent},
  {path: '**', component: NotFoundComponent}
]);
```

Lastly in App Module, make sure that you have imported the new component and add it to *declarations* array as shown below.

```
import { YourOwnComponent } from './your-own.component';
...

@NgModule({
  declarations: [
    AppComponent,
    HomeComponent,
    NotFoundComponent,
    GitHubComponent,
    YourOwnComponent
  ],
```

10.4 Route Parameters

We will now illustrate how to create routes that takes in route parameters. Why do we need this? For example, from the GitHub results page, we want to navigate to a page to see the details of a specific GitHub user, we can pass in the information via route parameters.

In app.routing.ts, we add a route that takes in two route parameters as shown below in **bold**.

```
import { NgModule } from '@angular/core';
import { Routes, RouterModule } from '@angular/router';

import { HomeComponent } from './home.component';
import { NotFoundComponent } from './notfound.component';
import { GitHubComponent } from './GitHub.component';
import { UserFormComponent } from './user-form.component';
```

```
import { GitHubUserComponent } from './githubuser.component';

export const routing = RouterModule.forRoot([
  {path: '', component: HomeComponent},
  {path: 'GitHub', component: GitHubComponent},
  {path: 'GitHub/user/:login/:score', component: GitHubUserComponent},
  {path: '**', component: NotFoundComponent}
]);
```

Code Explanation

We first import the GitHubUserComponent which we will implement later. The GitHubUserComponent simply displays some information about a specific GitHub User.

Next, we add a route

```
{path: 'GitHub/user/:login/:score', component: GitHubUserComponent}
```

/:login/:score represents the *login* route parameter and the *score* route parameter. If we want to pass in only one parameter for e.g. *login*, it will be just *GitHub/user/:login*. We can pass in multiple parameters (more than two) if we want to.

With this route, whenever we navigate to a url for e.g.

```
http://localhost:4200/GitHub/user/gregkh/45.82885
```

Angular will render the GitHubUserComponent with the parameter *login* 'gregkh' and *score* '45.82885'.

You might ask, why is our route *GitHub/user/:login/:score* and not *user/:login/:score*? That is because our GitHub search results are displayed in http://localhost:4200/GitHub/. If our search results are displayed in the root i.e. http://localhost:4200/, then our route will be *user/:login/:score*. We will explore different techniques to handle such routing later in the **Feature Routes** section.

Specifying Route Parameters

Next, in the template of github.component.ts, we add the line in **bold**.

```
  template: `
    <input class="form-control" type="search"
      [formControl]="searchControl">
    <div *ngIf="isLoading">
      <i class="fa fa-spinner fa-spin fa-3x"></i>
    </div>
    <h3>GitHub User Results</h3>
```

117

```
<div *ngIf="isLoading">
  <i class="fa fa-spinner fa-spin fa-3x"></i>
</div>
<div *ngFor="let user of users" class="media">
    <div class="media-left">
        <a [routerLink]="['user',user.login, user.score]">
        <img class="media-object img"
          src="{{ user.avatar_url }}" alt="...">
        </a>
    </div>
    <div class="media-body">
        <h4 class="media-heading">{{ user.login }}</h4>
        Score: {{ user.score }}
    </div>
</div> `,
```

Code Explanation

```
<a [routerLink]="['user',user.login, user.score]">
<img class="media-object img"
  src="{{ user.avatar_url }}" alt="...">
</a>
```

We add a *routerLink* to the user image of each search result. When one clicks on the user image, she will be routed to GitHubUserComponent with parameters *login* and *score*.

```
<a [routerLink]="['user',user.login, user.score]">
```

We use property binding syntax to bind our route parameters array to *routerLink*.

['user',user.login, user.score] is our route parameters array. The first element is a string which contains our path *user*. The second and third element are our route parameter values. If our route had more parameters, we could add them like *['user',user.login, user.score, artist.html_url]*

Retrieving Route Parameters

Next, we create GitHubUserComponent that shows the details of a particular user. In our case, we will just show the login and score of the user. Create and fill in githubuser.component.ts with the below code.

```
import { Component, OnInit } from '@angular/core';
import { ActivatedRoute } from '@angular/router';

@Component({
    selector: 'user',
```

118

```
    template: `
        <h1>User Login: {{ login }}</h1>
        <h2>User Score: {{ score }}</h2>`
})
export class GitHubUserComponent implements OnInit {
    login;
    score;
    subscription;

    constructor(private _route: ActivatedRoute){
    }

    ngOnInit(){
        this.subscription = this._route.params.subscribe(params => {
            this.login = params["login"];
            this.score = params["score"];
        })
    }
}
```

Code Explanation

```
@Component({
    selector: 'user',
    template: `
        <h1>User Login: {{ login }}</h1>
        <h2>User Score: {{ score }}</h2>`
})
```

In the template, we use string interpolation to display *login* and *score*. But how do we get the route parameters?

```
    constructor(private _route: ActivatedRoute){
    }
```

First, we use dependency injection to get an instance of *ActivatedRoute*. *ActivatedRoute* contains route information of a component and we subscribe to its params method to get our route parameters.

```
    ngOnInit(){
        this.subscription = this._route.params.subscribe(params => {
            this.login = params["login"];
            this.score = params["score"];
        })
    }
```

We implement the *ngOnInit* method (remember to implement *OnInit* in the class definition) and in it subscribe to *_route.params* which returns an Observable. We then get the value of the parameters using:

```
this.login = params["login"];
this.score = params["score"];
```

Additionally, to improve on memory, we can implement *ngOnDestroy()* so that we remove the subscription object from memory when this component instance is destroyed. See the complete code below with the *OnDestroy* code in **bold**.

```
import { Component, OnInit, OnDestroy } from '@angular/core';
import { ActivatedRoute } from '@angular/router';

@Component({
    selector: 'user',
    template: `
        <h1>User Login: {{ login }}</h1>
        <h2>User Score: {{ score }}</h2>
    `
})
export class GitHubUserComponent implements OnInit, OnDestroy {
    login;
    score;
    subscription;

    constructor(private _route: ActivatedRoute){
    }

    ngOnInit(){
        this.subscription = this._route.params.subscribe(params => {
            this.login = params["login"];
            this.score = params["score"];
        })
    }

    ngOnDestroy(){
        this.subscription.unsubscribe();
    }
}
```

Lastly, remember to import GitHubUserComponent and add it to *declarations* in app.module.ts as shown below in **bold**.

```
import { BrowserModule } from '@angular/platform-browser';
import { NgModule } from '@angular/core';
import { FormsModule } from '@angular/forms';
```

```
import { HttpClientModule } from '@angular/common/http';
...

import { GitHubUserComponent } from './githubuser.component';
import { routing } from './app.routing';

@NgModule({
  declarations: [
    AppComponent,
    HomeComponent,
    NotFoundComponent,
    GitHubComponent,
    GitHubUserComponent
  ],
  imports: [
    BrowserModule,
    FormsModule,
    ReactiveFormsModule,
    HttpClientModule,
    routing
  ],
  providers: [],
  bootstrap: [AppComponent]
})
export class AppModule { }
```

10.5 Imperative Navigation

Suppose we want to redirect a user to another page upon clicking a button or upon clicking submit in a form. In such a case, we cannot use *routerLink* directive. Instead, we need to talk to the router object directly and this is what we called imperative or programmatic navigation.

The below codes in <u>home.component.ts</u> illustrate this:

```
import { Component } from '@angular/core';
import { Router } from '@angular/router';

@Component({
    template: `
        <h1>Home</h1>
        <button (click)="onClick()">Go to GitHub Users</button>

`
})
export class HomeComponent {
```

```
    constructor(private _router: Router){

    }

    onClick(){
        this._router.navigate(['GitHub']);
    }
}
```

Code Explanation

```
        <button (click)="onClick()">Go to GitHub Users</button>
```

In the template, we have a **Go to GitHub Users** button and we do event binding to bind it to the *onClick()* method.

```
constructor(private _router: Router){
}
```

Next, we import and inject *Router* into the constructor of HomeComponent.

```
    onClick(){
        this._router.navigate(['GitHub']);
    }
```

In the *onClick* method, we call the *navigate* method of *Router* which takes in a route parameters array similar to the routes we have implemented earlier. The first element of the array will be the name of the target route and we supply any parameters in the second element of the array.

10.6 Route Guards

In a SPA, we may need to protect routes for example, preventing users from accessing areas that they're not allowed to access, or asking them for confirmation when leaving a certain area. Angular's router provides Route Guards that try to solve this problem.

There are two interfaces *CanActivate* and *CanDeactivate* which we can use to protect our routes. We use *CanActivate* to control if a user is allowed to navigate to a path, where certain pages are allowed only to logged-in users or users with certain permissions or role. We use *CanDeactivate* to display a confirmation box to the user and ask if they really want to navigate away for example, if they have entered values into a form and tries to navigate away before saving the changes.

We refer to *CanActivate* and *CanDeactivate* as Route Guards because they act as guards to routes. We implement Route Guards in a separate service class and apply this service class on the routes we want to guard.

RouteGuard CanActivate

Suppose we want to let users access the GitHub page only if they have logged in. In *app*, create a new file auth-guard.service.ts with the following codes.

```
import { Injectable } from '@angular/core';
import { CanActivate } from '@angular/router';

@Injectable()
export class AuthGuard implements CanActivate {

  canActivate(){
    return false;
  }

}
```

In the above code, we have currently set *canActivate()* to always return *false* and user will therefore never be able to access the page with this guard applied.

app.routing.ts

Next in app.routing.ts, add the codes in **bold**.

```
import { NgModule } from '@angular/core';
import { Routes, RouterModule } from '@angular/router';

import { HomeComponent } from './home.component';
import { NotFoundComponent } from './notfound.component';
import { GitHubComponent } from './users/user-form.component';

import { AuthGuard } from './auth-guard.service';

export const routing = RouterModule.forRoot([
  {path: '', component: HomeComponent},
  {path: 'GitHub',
      component: GitHubComponent,
      canActivate: [AuthGuard]},
  {path: 'GitHub/user/:login/:score', component: GitHubUserComponent},

  {path: '**', component: NotFoundComponent}
]);
```

Code Explanation

```
canActivate: [AuthGuard]}
```

We import and add the parameter *canActivate* to the *signup* route. *canActivate* takes in an array of guards, which means we can apply multiple guards to a given route if needed. If the first one returns false, the execution stops there. Otherwise, control is passed to the next guard. For now, we pass in an array with a single guard element *AuthGuard*.

If we run the app now, and you try to navigate to **GitHub**, nothing will happen and you will remain on the current page. This is because our route guard is at work here preventing access.

User Login

Now, how do we know if a user is currently logged in or not? Back in chapter 7, we implemented a separate login service class and component for authentication. The class had a *login* method. We further enhance the login class by adding a *logout* method and a boolean field *isLoggedIn* that tells us if a user is logged in or not.

The complete code for login.service.ts in app folder is shown below.

```
import {Injectable} from '@angular/core';
import {CanActivate} from '@angular/router';

@Injectable()
export class LoginService {
  isLoggedIn = false;

  login(username, password){
    if(username === "jason" && password === "123")
        this.isLoggedIn = true;
    else
        this.isLoggedIn = false;

    return this.isLoggedIn;
  }

  logout(){
      this.isLoggedIn = false;
      return this.isLoggedIn;
  }
}
```

As shown previously, the login service class is a simple plain Typescript class used behind our login form component. The values of *username* and *password* come in from the login form. In a real world application, *login()* should call a remote service with username/password and await a *true* or *false* return value. In this instance to simplify things, we will not be calling a remote service but instead hard code a specific username and password for successful login.

For the *logout* method, we don't call a remote service because the server is not aware if a user is logged in or not. This will be the client's responsibility which falls in the scope of Angular.

Do note that this is a basic implementation of an authentication service and in a real world application, you would probably have additional security measures like using encryption libraries to encrypt username/password and so on. We will next use this in our route guard, so back from the code in chapter 7, add login.service.ts, login.component.ts, login.component.ts and passwordValidator.ts to your project if you have not already done so. You can also refer to my sample code in GitHub to get the code for these classes.

auth-guard.service.ts

Back in auth-guard.service.ts, add the following codes in **bold**.

```
import { Injectable } from '@angular/core';
import { CanActivate, Router } from '@angular/router';
import { LoginService } from './login.service';

@Injectable()
export class AuthGuard implements CanActivate {

  constructor(private _loginService: LoginService,
              private _router:Router){
  }

  canActivate(){
    if(this._loginService.isLoggedIn)
      return true;

    // imperative navigation
    this._router.navigate(['login'])

    return false;
  }

}
```

We import *Router* and *LoginService* and use dependency injection to get an instance of these two classes. In *canActivate()*, we then check if *isLoggedIn* in *loginService* is true. If yes, return *true* and allow the route to continue the navigation. If *isLoggedIn* is *false*, navigate to the login page and return *false* so that that the request page remains inaccessible.

app.routing.ts

Next in app.routing.ts, we import and apply the *auth-guard* route guard to our routes for Home, GitHub, GitHubUser as shown below in **bold**. We also add the *login* route.

```
import { NgModule } from '@angular/core';
import { Routes, RouterModule } from '@angular/router';

import { HomeComponent } from './home.component';
import { NotFoundComponent } from './notfound.component';
import { GitHubComponent } from './github.component';
import { GitHubUserComponent } from './githubuser.component';

import { LoginComponent } from './login.component';
import { AuthGuard } from './auth-guard.service';

export const routing = RouterModule.forRoot([
  {path: '', component: HomeComponent, canActivate: [AuthGuard]},
  {path: 'GitHub', component: GitHubComponent, canActivate: [AuthGuard]},
  {path: 'GitHub/user/:login/:score', component: GitHubUserComponent,
canActivate: [AuthGuard]},
  {path: 'login', component: LoginComponent},
  {path: '**', component: NotFoundComponent}
]);
```

AppModule

Lastly, remember to register *AuthGuard, LoginService* in *providers* and *LoginComponent* in *declarations* of AppModule if you have not already done so.

Running the App

If you run your app now and try to access either Home, GitHub or GitHubUser, you will be directed to the login form. And when you sign in with 'jason' and '123', you will be able to access the pages.

If for any reason you cannot get your app to run, contact me at support@i-ducate.com.

RouteGuard CanDeactivate

We will illustrate implementing our *CanDeactivate* route guard on our login page. That is, when a user has entered values into the login form and tries to navigate away, we will prompt a pop up message 'Are you sure' first before confirming user decision to navigate away.

We implement our *CanDeactivate* route guard in a separate service class. In *app*, add a new file prevent-unsaved-changes-guard.service.ts.

```
import { CanDeactivate} from '@angular/router';
import { LoginComponent } from './login.component';

export class PreventUnsavedChangesGuard implements
CanDeactivate<LoginComponent>{

  canDeactivate(component: LoginComponent){
    if(component.form.dirty)
      return confirm("Are you sure?");

    return true;
  }
}
```

We implement the *canDeactivate* method and in it, we check if the form's *dirty* property which indicates if any of its form controls have been filled in. If yes, pop up the confirmation box. Else let the navigation away continue.

app.routing.ts

Next in app.routing.ts, apply the guard *PreventUnsavedChangesGuard* to the *login* route.

```
...
import { PreventUnsavedChangesGuard } from './prevent-unsaved-changes-
guard.service';

export const routing = RouterModule.forRoot([
  {path: '', component: HomeComponent, canActivate: [AuthGuard]},
  {path: 'GitHub', component: GitHubComponent, canActivate: [AuthGuard]},
  {path: 'GitHub/user/:login/:score', component: GitHubUserComponent,
      canActivate: [AuthGuard]},
  {path: 'login', component: LoginComponent, canDeactivate:
      [PreventUnsavedChangesGuard]},
  {path: '**', component: NotFoundComponent}
]);
```

AppModule

Remember to register *PreventUnsavedChangesGuard* in the *providers* array in AppModule.

Running the App

Now run the app and enter some values into the login form fields. Try navigating away and you should see the below pop up box confirmation your decision.

Summary

In this chapter, we see how to build single page apps with routing. We learnt how to define and configure routes, rendering requested component using the router outlet, providing router links, how to create routes with parameters, how to retrieve the parameters, using route guards for authorization with the *CanActivate* interface and preventing unsaved changes with the *CanDeactivate* interface.

We have covered a lot in this chapter. Contact me at support@i-ducate.com if you have not already had the full source code for this chapter or if you encounter any errors with your code.

CHAPTER 11: STRUCTURING LARGE APPS WITH MODULES

The application we have built in chapter nine and ten so far has three main function areas. The Home page, GitHub page and Login page. But once our app grows, maintenance becomes more important and challenging. It is then better to divide a large app into smaller parts each focusing on one specific functionality. Each part will have a group of highly related classes that work together to fulfil a specific function.

Gmail for example is a huge application. In it, we find different functionalities like Inbox, Contacts and Compose. Each function would have been formed from their own set of highly related classes which we term as one module.

In Angular, each application has at least one module, which is our main or root module **App Module**. We so far have been adding our components to this single root module.

But as our app grows, we should refactor this into smaller and more focused modules for better maintainability.

For example, in our application, our module directory will look something like:

```
/AppModule
  /GitHubModule
  /LoginModule
  ...
```

11.1 NgModule

A module is just a class decorated with the *NgModule* decorator. We already saw it in app.module.ts in chapter 10 and earlier chapters (shortened code snippet shown below).

```
import ...

@NgModule({
  declarations: [
    AppComponent,
    HomeComponent,
    NotFoundComponent,
    GitHubComponent,
```

```
    GitHubUserComponent,
    LoginComponent
  ],
  imports: [
    BrowserModule,
    FormsModule,
    ReactiveFormsModule,
    HttpClientModule,
    routing
  ],
  providers: [
    LoginService,
    AuthGuard,
    PreventUnsavedChangesGuard
],
  bootstrap: [AppComponent]
})
export class AppModule { }
```

As mentioned earlier, the *imports* array specify what other modules this present module depends on. We can see that the above AppModule depends on BrowserModule, FormsModule, ReactiveFormsModule, HttpClientModule and our routing Module.

The *declarations* array specify what components, directives and pipes are part of this module. We currently have AppComponent, HomeComponent, NotFoundComponent, GitHubComponent, GitHubUserComponent, LoginComponent as part of AppModule.

We specify the boot or entry module in the *bootstrap* array of our app. We have specified AppComponent as the entry point for our application. Note that this is only required in the root module AppModule and not needed in the sub-modules we create.

The *providers* array specify mainly service classes that we use through dependency injection.

So what is the benefit of listing components and services in these arrays? The benefit is that we don't have to individually import components for every other component in the same module. For e.g. in GitHubComponent, we already have access to GitHubUserComponent without importing it since it is declared to be in the same module. So as long as components are in the same module, they will be available to one another in the module. This results in much cleaner code where we don't have to keep repeating similar import statements in multiple classes.

11.2 Restructuring

Our AppModule now is beginning to get quite huge and messy. Currently, all files are in one single module. So how do we re-structure it into smaller, focused modules like in the below structure?

```
/AppModule
  /GitHubModule
  /LoginModule
  ...
```

We will try to refactor some classes out from AppModule to form GitHubModule and LoginModule. The related classes for GitHubModule will be GitHubComponent, GitHubUserComponent and GitHubService.

The related classes for LoginModule will be LoginComponent, LoginService, PasswordValidator, AuthGuard and PreventUnsavedChangesGuard.

HomeComponent and NotFoundComponent will remain in AppModule since they are generic to the application.

In our existing project folder from chapter ten, create two new folders *github* and *login* in */app*. So that the folder structure looks like below:

```
/app
  /github
  /login
...
```

Restructuring GitHubModule

We first refactor for GitHubModule. Move the below files from */app* to */app/github*

github.component.ts
githubuser.component.ts
github.service.ts

In */app/github*, create github.module.ts with the below code.

```
import { NgModule }             from '@angular/core';
import { CommonModule }         from '@angular/common';
import { ReactiveFormsModule } from '@angular/forms';
import { RouterModule }         from '@angular/router';
import { HttpClientModule }        from '@angular/common/http';

import { GitHubComponent }    from './github.component';
import { GitHubUserComponent }     from './githubuser.component';
import { GitHubService }        from './github.service';
```

131

```
@NgModule({
    imports: [
        CommonModule,
        ReactiveFormsModule,
        HttpClientModule,
        RouterModule
    ],
    declarations: [
        GitHubComponent,
        GitHubUserComponent
    ],
    exports: [
    ],
    providers: [
        GitHubService
    ]
})
export class GitHubModule {
}
```

Code Explanation

Notice that github.module.ts is very much similar to app.module.ts except that it contains files specific to the GitHub Module which we store in a separate GitHub folder.

A difference is that we import CommonModule instead of BrowserModule. In an Angular app, only the root application module AppModule should import BrowserModule. BrowserModule provides services that are essential to launch and run a browser app. Feature modules (or sub-modules) should import CommonModule instead. They need the common directives and don't need to re-install the app-wide providers.

Restructuring LoginModule

Next, we refactor for LoginModule. Move the below files from /*app* to /*app*/*login*.

login.component.ts
login.component.html
login.service.ts
passwordValidator.ts
auth-guard.service.ts
prevent-unsaved-changes-guard.service.ts

In /*app*/*login*/, create login.module.ts with the below code.

```
import { NgModule }                from '@angular/core';
```

```
import { CommonModule }        from '@angular/common';
import { FormsModule } from '@angular/forms';
import { ReactiveFormsModule } from '@angular/forms';
import { LoginComponent }  from './login.component';
import { LoginService }  from './login.service';
import { PreventUnsavedChangesGuard } from './prevent-unsaved-changes-guard.service';
import { AuthGuard } from './auth-guard.service';

@NgModule({
    imports: [
        CommonModule,
        FormsModule,
        ReactiveFormsModule
    ],
    declarations: [
        LoginComponent
    ],
    exports: [
    ],
    providers: [
        LoginService,
        PreventUnsavedChangesGuard,
        AuthGuard
    ]
})
export class LoginModule {
}
```

Restructuring AppModule

Because we have already imported ReactiveFormsModule, HttpClientModule, RouterModule in GitHubModule and FormsModule in LoginModule, we can remove them from AppModule.

Similarly, because we have imported GitHubComponent, GitHubUserComponent, GitHubService in GitHubModule, LoginComponent, LoginService, AuthGuard, PreventUnsavedChangesGuard in LoginModule, we can remove the *import* and *provider* statements for these classes from AppModule as shown below. Instead, we import GitHubModule and LoginModule.

app.module.ts

133

```
import { BrowserModule } from '@angular/platform-browser';
import { NgModule } from '@angular/core';

import { AppComponent } from './app.component';
import { HomeComponent } from './home.component';
import { NotFoundComponent } from './notfound.component';

import { routing } from './app.routing';
import { AuthGuard } from './auth-guard.service';
import { PreventUnsavedChangesGuard } from './prevent-unsaved-changes-guard.service';

import { GitHubModule } from './github/github.module';
import { LoginModule } from './login/login.module';

@NgModule({
  declarations: [
    AppComponent,
    HomeComponent,
    NotFoundComponent,
  ],
  imports: [
    BrowserModule,
    LoginModule,
    GitHubModule,
    routing
  ],
  providers: [
  ],
  bootstrap: [AppComponent]
})
export class AppModule { }
```

Realize that after refactoring, AppModule becomes much smaller? We only make code changes to AppModule when we add new modules to it. And both GitHubModule and LoginModule can grow on its own. We can add new classes, components, pipes, directives to them without impacting AppModule. This is the benefit of modularity.

Finally in app.routing.ts, do the below minor changes in **bold**. This is because we have moved GitHub related components to *github* folder and LoginComponent to *login* folder.

```
import { NgModule } from '@angular/core';
import { Routes, RouterModule } from '@angular/router';

import { HomeComponent } from './home.component';
import { NotFoundComponent } from './notfound.component';
```

134

```
import { GitHubComponent } from './github/github.component';
import { GitHubUserComponent } from './github/githubuser.component';

import { LoginComponent } from './login/login.component';
import { AuthGuard } from './login/auth-guard.service';

import { PreventUnsavedChangesGuard } from './login/prevent-unsaved-
changes-guard.service';

export const routing = RouterModule.forRoot([
...
]);
```

11.3 Restructuring Routes

Although app.module.ts has been structured to be more modular, app.routing.ts still contains all the routes in a single file. If the number of routes increases to hundreds or thousands, app.routing.ts will become messy and unmaintainable. So just as we have refactored app.module.ts, we can also divide our routes into smaller more manageable routing files.

With this structure, instead of having a gigantic app.routing.ts with hundreds of routes, we will have a feature route file per module and app.routing.ts will delegate all the routing for that module to that feature routing file.

That is, we move routes in a feature area to its corresponding module. For example, we move the below two routes to their own GitHub Module routing file.

```
{path: 'GitHub', component: GitHubComponent, canActivate: [AuthGuard]},
{path: 'GitHub/user/:login/:score', component: GitHubUserComponent,
canActivate: [AuthGuard]},
```

In GitHub folder, add a new file github.routing.ts with the below code. This will be the routing file for GitHub Module.

```
import { NgModule } from '@angular/core';
import { Routes, RouterModule } from '@angular/router';
import { GitHubComponent } from './github.component';
import { GitHubUserComponent } from './githubuser.component';
import { AuthGuard } from '../login/auth-guard.service';

export const GitHubRouting = RouterModule.forChild([
  {path: 'GitHub', component: GitHubComponent, canActivate: [AuthGuard]},
  {path: 'GitHub/user/:login/:score', component: GitHubUserComponent,
canActivate: [AuthGuard]},
```

```
]);
```

app.routing.ts

app.routing.ts will have the below code. Note that the GitHub related routes have been removed resulting in cleaner and modular code.

```
import { NgModule } from '@angular/core';
import { Routes, RouterModule } from '@angular/router';

import { HomeComponent } from './home.component';
import { NotFoundComponent } from './notfound.component';

import { LoginComponent } from './login/login.component';
import { AuthGuard } from './login/auth-guard.service';

import { PreventUnsavedChangesGuard } from './login/prevent-unsaved-
changes-guard.service';

export const routing = RouterModule.forRoot([
  {path: '', component: HomeComponent, canActivate: [AuthGuard]},
  {path: 'login', component: LoginComponent, canDeactivate:
[PreventUnsavedChangesGuard]},
  {path: '**', component: NotFoundComponent}
]);
```

app.module.ts

app.module.ts will have the below code changes in **bold**.

```
import { BrowserModule } from '@angular/platform-browser';
import { NgModule } from '@angular/core';

import { AppComponent } from './app.component';
import { HomeComponent } from './home.component';
import { NotFoundComponent } from './notfound.component';

import { LoginModule } from './login/login.module';
import { GitHubModule } from './github/github.module';

import { routing } from './app.routing';
import { GitHubRouting } from './github/github.routing'

@NgModule({
  declarations: [
    AppComponent,
```

136

```
    HomeComponent,
    NotFoundComponent
  ],
  imports: [
    BrowserModule,
    LoginModule,
    GitHubModule,
    GitHubRouting,
    routing
  ],
  providers: [

  ],
  bootstrap: [AppComponent]
})
export class AppModule { }
```

Here, we import both our routing modules into AppModule. Notice that in the *imports* array, we import *GitHubRouting* before *routing*. We should **NOT** import *routing* before *GitHubRouting* as shown below:

```
  imports: [
    BrowserModule,
    LoginModule,
    GitHubModule,
    routing,
    GitHubRouting
  ],
```

If we do this, *routing* will be processed first meaning that links to GitHub and GitHubUser component will be directed to NotFoundComponent instead. We should instead have *GitHubRouting* imported first to avoid this.

Summary

In this chapter, we covered how to refactor our application as it grows, into smaller and more focused modules for better maintainability. We learnt how to declare a module with the NgModule decorator, how to refactor files into separate module folder structures and also how to refactor routes to their own modules.

CHAPTER 12: C.R.U.D. WITH FIREBASE/FIRESTORE

In this chapter, we will cover how to implement full C.R.U.D. operations in Angular with a backend server. A typical web application architecture consists of the server side and client side. This book teaches you how to implement the client side using Angular. The client side talks to a backend server to get or save data via RESTful http services built using server side frameworks like ASP.NET, Node.js and Ruby on Rails. We had explored this when we got data from the GitHub server in chapter nine.

Building the server side, however is often time consuming and not within the scope of this course. In this chapter, however, we will explore using Firebase as our backend server. Firebase is Google's real-time database which offers a very powerful backend platform for building fast and scalable real-time apps.

With Firebase, we don't have to write server side code or design relational databases. Firebase provides us with a real-time, fast and scalable database in the cloud and also a library to talk to this database. This allows us to focus on building our application according to requirements rather than debugging server side code.

Firebase stores our data in objects called *documents* which are grouped into *collections*. Within these collections, you can have more sub-collections up to hundred levels deep. You can then query for the *documents* with *where* clauses.

This chapter aims to, however, illustrate create, read, update and delete functionality with Angular and Firebase integrated so that you can go on and create a fully working app. And if you choose to have a different backend server like ASP.NET, Node.js, the same principles will apply.

More on Firebase

Firebase is a real time database. which means that as data is modified, all connected clients are automatically refreshed in an optimised way. If one user adds a new item either through a browser or a mobile app, another user (again either through a browser or mobile app) sees the addition in real time without refreshing the page. Firebase of course provides more than just a real time database. It provides other services like Authentication, cloud messaging, disk space, hosting an analytics. You not only can develop Angular apps with Firestore as backend, but also iOS, Android and web applications.

12.1 Using Firebase

We can use Firebase features for free and only pay when our application grows bigger. You can choose between a subscription based or 'pay as you use' model. Find out more at firebase.google.com/pricing.

Before adding Firebase to our Angular project, we need to first create a Firebase account. Go to firebase.google.com and sign in with your Google account.

Click **'Get Started'** to go to the Firebase console. In the console, click on 'Add Project' (figure 12.1)

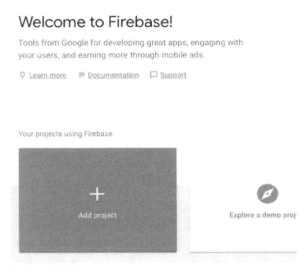

figure 12.1.1

Fill in the project name, country and click 'Create Project'.

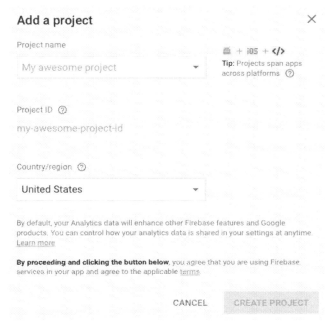

figure 12.1.2

In the Welcome screen, click on 'Add Firebase to your web app' (figure 12.3).

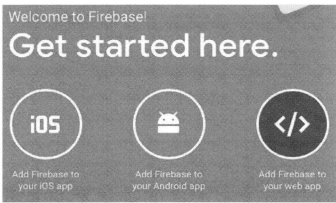

figure 12.1.3

You will see some configuration code that you need to add in your project (fig. 12.1.4).

Add Firebase to your web app ✕

Copy and paste the snippet below at the bottom of your HTML, before other `script` tags.

```
<script src="https://www.gstatic.com/firebasejs/4.8.0/firebase.js"></script>
<script>
  // Initialize Firebase
  var config = {
    apiKey: "AIzaSyAJJsAt0ioATHVrZFACTMs_BXKP1lypvbc",
    authDomain: "myfirestore-379ff.firebaseapp.com",
    databaseURL: "https://myfirestore-379ff.firebaseio.com",
    projectId: "myfirestore-379ff",
    storageBucket: "myfirestore-379ff.appspot.com",
    messagingSenderId: "24164266017"
  };
  firebase.initializeApp(config);
</script>
```

COPY

figure 12.1.4

Code Explanation

```
<script src="https://www.gstatic.com/firebasejs/4.8.0/firebase.js"></script>
```

This is a script reference to Firebase SDK. firebase.js gives us a library to work with firebase.

```
<script>
  // Initialize Firebase
  var config = {
    apiKey: "AIzaSyAJJsAt0ioATHVrZFACTMs_BXKP1lypvbc",
    authDomain: "myfirestore-379ff.firebaseapp.com",
    databaseURL: "https://myfirestore-379ff.firebaseio.com",
    projectId: "myfirestore-379ff",
    storageBucket: "myfirestore-379ff.appspot.com",
    messagingSenderId: "24164266017"
  };
  firebase.initializeApp(config);
</script>
```

We have a *config* or configuration object with properties *apiKey*, *authDomain* (a subdomain under firebaseapp.com), *databaseUrl*, *storageBucket* (for storing files like photos, videos etc.) and *messagingSenderId* (used for sending push notifications).

12.2 Adding Firebase to our Angular App

To illustrate connecting Firebase to our Angular app, we will create a new project using Angular CLI (I have named my project CRUDProject and remember to add the bootstrap link in index.html).

```
ng new CRUDProject
```

We will next use *npm* to add firebase and another library called *angularfire* to our project.

```
npm install firebase angularfire2 --save
```

After the installation, in package.json, an entry for firebase will have been added (see lines below in **bold**).

```
"dependencies": {
  "@angular/animations": "^5.0.0",
  "@angular/common": "^5.0.0",
  "@angular/compiler": "^5.0.0",
  "@angular/core": "^5.0.0",
  "@angular/forms": "^5.0.0",
  "@angular/http": "^5.0.0",
  "@angular/platform-browser": "^5.0.0",
  "@angular/platform-browser-dynamic": "^5.0.0",
  "@angular/router": "^5.0.0",
  "angularfire2": "^5.0.0-rc.4",
  "core-js": "^2.4.1",
  "firebase": "^4.7.0",
  "rxjs": "^5.1.0",
  "zone.js": "^0.8.4"
},
```

(Note: At time of writing, this chapter uses AngularFire Version 5)

app.module.ts

As of AngularFire2 5.0.0, we need to import *AngularFireModule* and also *AngularFirestoreModule* into App Module. In app.module.ts, add the lines in **bold**. Note that the credential properties in *firebaseConfig* should be your own (copied from firebase console)

```
import { BrowserModule } from '@angular/platform-browser';
import { NgModule } from '@angular/core';
import { AppComponent } from './app.component';

import { AngularFireModule} from 'angularfire2';
import { AngularFirestoreModule } from 'angularfire2/firestore';

var config = {
  apiKey: "AIzaSyBFn-c8pyMoTxeEOKlIZpFbeaTlHW4raAY",
  authDomain: "firestore-50589.firebaseapp.com",
```

143

```
    databaseURL: "https://firestore-50589.firebaseio.com",
    projectId: "firestore-50589",
    storageBucket: "firestore-50589.appspot.com",
    messagingSenderId: "31750657780"
};

@NgModule({
  declarations: [
    AppComponent
  ],
  imports: [
    BrowserModule,
    AngularFireModule.initializeApp(config),
    AngularFirestoreModule,
  ],
  providers: [],
  bootstrap: [AppComponent]
})
export class AppModule { }
```

We import a couple of libraries that sit on top of firebase and makes it easier to build Angular apps that use firebase. We then add these libraries to our *imports* section.

app.component.ts

Now to make sure that we have added firebase correctly to our project, go to app.component.ts and add the lines in **bold**.

```
import { Component } from '@angular/core';
import { AngularFirestore } from 'angularfire2/firestore';

@Component({
  selector: 'app-root',
  template: ``
})
export class AppComponent {
  constructor(private afs: AngularFirestore){
    console.log(afs);
  }
}

export class AppComponent {
```

Now, make sure that the lite web server is running, (by executing *ng serve*) and in the console, you should see the *AngularFirestore* object printed as shown below to prove that we have added Angular Fire correctly.

144

```
                                    app.component.ts:10
▼AngularFirestore {app: FirebaseAppImpl, firestore: Firestore, pe
  ▶app: FirebaseAppImpl {firebase_: {…}, isDeleted_: false, servic
  ▶firestore: Firestore {_queue: AsyncQueue, INTERNAL: {…}, _conf:
  ▶persistenceEnabled$: PromiseObservable {_isScalar: false, prom:
  ▶__proto__: Object
```

12.3 Working with a Firebase Database

Now let's look at our Firebase database. Go to console.firebase.google.com. Click on your project, and from the menu bar on the left, click on **Database**. Choose '**Try Firestore Beta**' as shown in fig. 12.3.1 (Note: It is currently in beta at the time of this writing, but that may have changed. This process should remain the same).

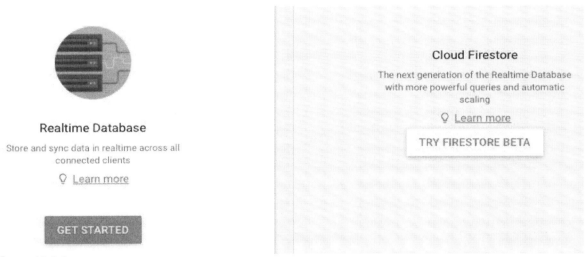

figure 12.3.1

On the next screen shown below (fig. 12.3.2), choose 'test mode' and then click 'Enable'.

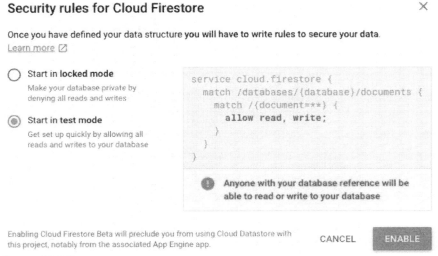

figure 12.3.2

On the next screen (fig. 12.3.3), click 'Add Collection' and name the collection 'users'.

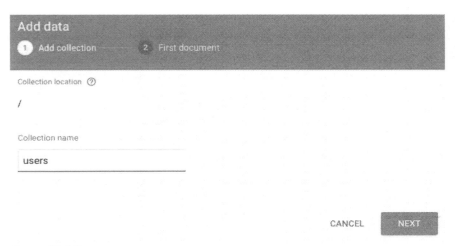

figure 12.3.3

Then, add two fields of type string (name, email) and provide them with some initial value (fig. 12.3.4).

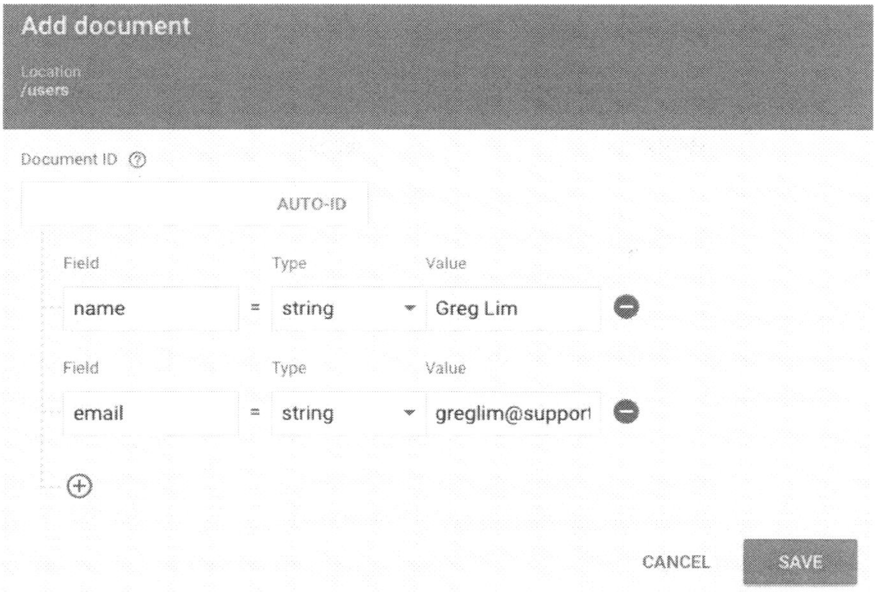

figure 12.3.4

Click 'save' when done.

So, in Firestore, we store our data in terms of collections and documents in these collections (fig. 12.3.5).

figure 12.3.5

Although we have specified a string type for our field, you can experiment with other primitive types like Boolean, number and even complex objects.

In the next sections, we will illustrate with a simple example of user objects in our Firebase database.

12.4 Displaying List of Users

We will illustrate how to display a list of users.

user.component.ts

First, we will create a user component to display our list of users. Create user.component.ts in *app* with the following code.

```
import { Component } from '@angular/core';
import {AngularFirestore, AngularFirestoreCollection,
AngularFirestoreDocument} from 'angularfire2/firestore';

interface User{
  name: string;
  email: string;
}
@Component({
    selector: 'users',
    templateUrl: './users.component.html'
  })
export class UsersComponent {

  usersCol: AngularFirestoreCollection<User>;
  users: any;

  constructor(private afs: AngularFirestore){
  }

  ngOnInit(){
    this.usersCol = this.afs.collection('users');
    this.users = this.usersCol.valueChanges();
  }
}
```

Code Explanation

```
import { AngularFireDatabase } from 'angularfire2/database';
import {AngularFirestore, AngularFirestoreCollection,
AngularFirestoreDocument} from 'angularfire2/firestore';
```

We import not only *AngularFirestore* but also *AngularFirestoreCollection* and *AngularFirestoreDocument*. We use them to interact with either the collections which store documents or to retrieve specific documents. For now, we focus on retrieving a collection first.

We define an interface *User* which helps us define the structure of the data associated with our *users* collection.

```
interface User{
  name: string;
  email: string;
}
```

In our class, we define two properties, *usersCol* which is of type *AngularFirestoreCollection* of type *User* (the interface defined above) and *users* which contains the array of *user* objects returned.

```
  usersCol: AngularFirestoreCollection<User>;
  users: any;
```

We then get an instance of *AngularFirestore* from injecting it in our constructor.

```
  constructor(private afs: AngularFirestore){
  }
```

In *ngOnInit*, we bind *usersCol* to our *AngularFirestore* instance with the *.collection* method where we pass in the name of our collection, 'users'.

```
  ngOnInit(){
    this.usersCol = this.afs.collection('users');
    this.users = this.usersCol.valueChanges();
  }
```

We then bind *users* to *usersCol.valueChanges()* which provides us with an Observable.

user.component.html

Next, create user.component.html with the below code:

```
<h1>Users</h1>
<table class="table table-bordered">
      <thead>
            <tr>
                  <th>Username</th>
                  <th>Email</th>
```

149

```
            <th>Edit</th>
            <th>Delete</th>
        </tr>
    </thead>
    <tbody>
        <tr *ngFor="let user of users | async">
            <td>{{ user.name }}</td>
            <td>{{ user.email }}</td>
            <td>
          <a>
              <i class="glyphicon glyphicon-edit"></i>
          </a>
            </td>
            <td>
          <a>
              <i class="glyphicon glyphicon-remove"></i>
          </a>
        </td>
        </tr>
    </tbody>
</table>
```

Code Explanation

```
<table class="table table-bordered">
```

We use the bootstrap classes *table* and *table-bordered* to create a nice looking table for listing our users.

```
        <a>
            <i class="glyphicon glyphicon-edit"></i>
        </a>
          </td>
          <td>
        <a>
            <i class="glyphicon glyphicon-remove"></i>
        </a>
```

We also use glyphicons *edit* and *remove* for the edit and delete operations we will implement later.

```
        <tr *ngFor="let user of users | async">
            <td>{{ user.name }}</td>
            <td>{{ user.email }}</td>
```

Notice that we have applied the *async* pipe in our *ngFor to display users. Because data in *users* arrive asynchronously, the *async* pipe subscribes to *user* (which is an Observable) and returns the latest value emitted. The *async* pipe marks the component to be checked for changes.

150

Before we try to run our app and display our list of users, we have to import and declare that *UsersComponent* belongs to App Module in app.module.ts.

app.module.ts

In app.module.ts, import UsersComponent with the below line:

```
import { UsersComponent } from './users.component';
```

and add it to *declarations* as shown below:

```
@NgModule({
  declarations: [
    AppComponent,
    UsersComponent
  ],
```

Adding Routing

app.routing.ts

To add routing to our project, create the routing file app.routing.ts in app as shown below.

```
import { RouterModule } from '@angular/router';
import { UsersComponent } from './users.component';

export const routing = RouterModule.forRoot([
    { path:'', component:UsersComponent }
]);
```

It currently contains only one route which points to User component. We will extend the routes later to include the route to the User Add and Edit form.

Remember to import and add *routing* to *imports* in app.module.ts.

```
import { routing } from './app.routing';
```

...

```
  imports: [
    BrowserModule,
    AngularFireModule.initializeApp(config),
    AngularFirestoreModule,
```

```
    routing
  ],
```

app.component.ts

Back in app.component.ts, we add *router-outlet* into the template as shown below to render our content.

```
import { Component } from '@angular/core';
import { AngularFirestore } from 'angularfire2/firestore';

@Component({
  selector: 'app-root',
  template: `
    <router-outlet></router-outlet>
  `
})
export class AppComponent {
  constructor(private afs: AngularFirestore){
    console.log(afs);
  }
}
```

To make the code cleaner, we also remove the previous logging code as shown in the strikethrough lines above.

index.html

Remember to add the bootstrap link in index.html as shown below to make sure that our table borders are rendered correctly.

```
<!doctype html>
<html lang="en">
<head>
  <meta charset="utf-8">
  <title>Firestore</title>
  <base href="/">

  <meta name="viewport" content="width=device-width, initial-scale=1">
  <link rel="icon" type="image/x-icon" href="favicon.ico">
  <link rel="stylesheet"
    href="https://maxcdn.bootstrapcdn.com/bootstrap/4.0.0/css/bootstrap.min.css"
integrity="sha384-
Gn5384xqQ1aoWXA+058RXPxPg6fy4IWvTNh0E263XmFcJlSAwiGgFAW/dAiS6JXm"
    crossorigin="anonymous">
</head>
<body>
  <app-root></app-root>
```

152

```
</body>
</html>
```

Running Your App

When you run your app now, you should see a list of users rendered as shown.

Users

Username	Email	Edit	Delete
Greg Lim	greglim@support.com	☑	✖
Jason	jason@lim.com	☑	✖
Cheryl	Email@email.com	☑	✖
wwww.ww	wwww@ww.ww	☑	✖

If you modify the name or email of an existing document, the result in the browser instantly changes. And if you add/delete a new document from the firebase console, the result is automatically reflected in realtime as well! That's the beauty of firebase. We achieved auto-refresh upon adding, updated and deleting.

12.5 Adding a User

users.component.html

Next, we will implement adding a user to our app. First, add a button called **Add User** just before the user list in users.component.html. Decorate it with css button classes *btn* and *btn-primary* as shown below.

```
<h1>Users</h1>
<button class="btn btn-primary" (click)="add()">Add</button>
<table class="table table-bordered">
...
```

users.component.ts

When we click this button, we route to a new page with a form to add a new user. To create this route, implement the *add()* method in user.component.ts as shown below.

```
import { Component } from '@angular/core';
import { AngularFirestore, AngularFirestoreCollection,
```

```
AngularFirestoreDocument} from 'angularfire2/firestore';
import { Router } from '@angular/router';

interface User{
  name: string;
  email: string;
}
@Component({
    selector: 'users',
    templateUrl: './users.component.html'
  })
export class UsersComponent {

  usersCol: AngularFirestoreCollection<User>;
  users: any;

  constructor(private afs: AngularFirestore, private _router: Router){

  }

  ngOnInit(){
    this.usersCol = this.afs.collection('users');
    this.users = this.usersCol.valueChanges();
  }

  add(){
    this._router.navigate(['add']);
  }
}
```

app.routing.ts

In app.routing.ts, import and add the path to UserForm component as shown below. We will create UserForm component in the next section.

```
import { RouterModule } from '@angular/router';
import { UsersComponent } from './users.component';
import { UserFormComponent } from './user-form.component';

export const routing = RouterModule.forRoot([
    { path:'', component:UsersComponent },
    { path:'add',component:UserFormComponent }
]);
```

user.ts

We represent the model data behind our User form with the class *User* in user.ts. So add this class in *app*.

```
export class User{
    name: string;
    email: string;
}
```

user-form.component.ts

Next, create a new component user-form.component.ts that implements a model driven form with fields, *username* and *email* as shown below.

```
import { Component } from '@angular/core';
import { FormBuilder, FormGroup, Validators } from '@angular/forms';
import { Router } from '@angular/router';
import { AngularFirestore, AngularFirestoreDocument} from
'angularfire2/firestore';

import { User } from './user';

@Component({
    selector:'user-form',
    templateUrl: 'user-form.component.html'
})
export class UserFormComponent  {
    form: FormGroup;
    title: string;
    user = new User();

    constructor(fb: FormBuilder, private _router:Router,
private afs: AngularFirestore){
        this.form = fb.group({
            username:['',Validators.required ],
            email:['',Validators.required]
        })
    }

    ngOnInit(){
        this.title = "New User";
    }

    submit(){
```

```
    this.afs.collection('users').add({
        name: this.user.name,
        email: this.user.email
    });
    this._router.navigate(['']);
  }
}
```

Code Explanation

The code pertaining to generating a model driven form should be familiar to you as explained in **chapter 7: Model Driven Forms**. We will provide a brief explanation in the following sections.

```
export class UserFormComponent   {
    form: FormGroup;
    title: string;
    user = new User();
```

We want to remind you that it is important to initialize *user* to be a blank *User* object to avoid any null reference exception that might occur in the loading of the form either when we add a new user or later when we reuse the form again to edit an existing user.

```
    this.form = fb.group({
            username:['',Validators.required ],
            email:['',Validators.required]
        })
```

We create our form using the FormBuilder object that has two controls, *username* and *email* (each having the *required* validator applied to it). You can of course implement and apply your own custom validators as we have gone through in chapter 7.

AngularFirestore Add

Here I would like to focus on the *submit()* method which will be called by the form upon submit.

```
    submit(){
        this.afs.collection('users').add({
            name: this.user.name,
            email: this.user.email
        });
        this._router.navigate(['']);
    }
```

To add an object to firebase, we use the *add* method from Angular Firestore collection which we covered earlier in listing users.

To be able to add an object to firebase, we need to have write permission. Earlier on, we had set this to be *true* in the firebase console when we selected the 'test mode' option.

After adding the new user, we navigate back to the list of users with *this._router.navigate([''])*.

user-form.component.html

Next, create the template of UserForm Component in user-form.component.html with the below codes.

```
<h1>{{ title }}</h1>
<form [formGroup]="form" (ngSubmit)="submit()">
    <div class="form-group">
        <label for="username">Username</label>
        <input [(ngModel)]="user.username" type="text" class="form-control"
            formControlName="username">
        <div *ngIf="form.controls.username.touched &&
            !form.controls.username.valid" class="alert alert-danger">
          Username is required
        </div>
    </div>
    <div class="form-group">
        <label for="email">Email</label>
        <input [(ngModel)]="user.email" class="form-control"
            formControlName="email">
        <div *ngIf="form.controls.email.touched && form.controls.email.errors">
            <div *ngIf="form.controls.email.errors.required"
                    class="alert alert-danger">
                Email is required.
            </div>
        </div>
    </div>
    <button [disabled]="!form.valid" class="btn btn-primary"
type="submit">{{ title }}</button>
</form>
```

Code Explanation

The markup for the form should be familiar to you. If not, go back to chapter 6 and 7 for a revision.

```
        <label for="username">Username</label>
        <input [(ngModel)]="user.username" type="text" class="form-control"
            formControlName="username">
        <div *ngIf="form.controls.username.touched &&
            !form.controls.username.valid" class="alert alert-danger">
```

```
        Username is required
    </div>
```

Essentially, we have done some basic validation to the username and email fields. If no username is supplied, we display an alert message "Username is required". If no email is supplied, we display the alert message "Email is required". We have also applied the *form-control* class to give our form the bootstrap looking feel.

```
<button [disabled]="!form.valid" class="btn btn-primary"
type="submit">{{ title }}</button>
```

We disable the **Submit** button till all fields are valid.

app.module.ts

Lastly, in app.module.ts, we import ReactiveFormsModule because we need it for model driven forms. We also import and declare UserForm Component to be part of App Module.

```
import { BrowserModule } from '@angular/platform-browser';
import { NgModule } from '@angular/core';
import { AppComponent } from './app.component';

import { AngularFireModule} from 'angularfire2';
import { AngularFirestoreModule } from 'angularfire2/firestore';

import { UsersComponent } from './users.component';
import { routing } from './app.routing';

import { ReactiveFormsModule } from '@angular/forms';
import { UserFormComponent } from './user-form.component';

var config = {
  apiKey: "AIzaSyBFn-c8pyMoTxeEOKlIZpFbeaTlHW4raAY",
  authDomain: "firestore-50589.firebaseapp.com",
  databaseURL: "https://firestore-50589.firebaseio.com",
  projectId: "firestore-50589",
  storageBucket: "firestore-50589.appspot.com",
  messagingSenderId: "31750657780"
};

@NgModule({
  declarations: [
    AppComponent,
    UsersComponent,
    UserFormComponent
  ],
```

```
  imports: [
    BrowserModule,
    AngularFireModule.initializeApp(config),
    AngularFirestoreModule,
    ReactiveFormsModule,
    routing
  ],
  providers: [],
  bootstrap: [AppComponent]
})
export class AppModule { }
```

Try it yourself

As an exercise, implement dirty tracking on the form. That is, if we fill out the fields in the form and accidentally navigate away from the form page, show a confirmation box warning us that we have unsaved changes. And we click *Cancel* to stay on the form or *Ok* to navigate away. We have explained this in **chapter 10** where we covered the *CanDeactivate* interface.

Running your app

Run your app now. Go to the **Add** form, enter in a new username and email and upon submitting the form, you should be able to see your new user object added to the list.

12.6a Retrieving a Single User and Deletion

Before we go on to implement operations like delete and edit user, we need access to a specific document. To do so, we will need the *id* of the user. The current *users* as returned by the below code does not contain the id for each user.

```
this.users = this.usersCol.valueChanges();
```

id is considered metadata. To get the metadata, we use *snapshotChanges* instead of *valueChanges* in ngOnInit as shown below in **bold**.

```
import { map } from 'rxjs/operators';
...

    ngOnInit(){
        this.usersCol = this.afs.collection('users');
        this.users = this.usersCol.snapshotChanges()
            .pipe(
```

```
        map(actions => {
            return actions.map( a => {
                const data = a.payload.doc.data() as User;
                const id = a.payload.doc.id;
                return { id, data};
            });
        })
    );
}
```

snapshotChanges() provides us with other metadata of the document like id. We provide a callback to *snapshotChanges* which provides us with the payload which is the document itself and the id which firebase assigns by default to a document.

Now because the document itself is passed to user.data, we need to make changes to users.component.html as shown:

```
<tr *ngFor="let user of users | async">
    <td>{{ user.data.name }}</td>
    <td>{{ user.data.email }}</td>
```

With this, we are ready to proceed with deleting a user.

12.6b Deleting a User

We want to delete a user by clicking on the delete icon in a row of the user list, and a confirmation box will appear asking us if we want to delete the user.

users.component.html

First in users.component.html, we bind the *click* event of the delete icon to the *delete()* method with the newly acquired *user.id* and *user.data.name* as argument.

```
<h1>Users</h1>
<button class="btn btn-primary" (click)="add()">Add</button>
<table class="table table-bordered">
    <thead>
        <tr>
            <th>Username</th>
            <th>Email</th>
            <th>Edit</th>
            <th>Delete</th>
        </tr>
    </thead>
```

```
    <tbody>
        <tr *ngFor="let user of users | async">
            <td>{{ user.data.name }}</td>
            <td>{{ user.data.email }}</td>
            <td>
        <a>
            <i class="glyphicon glyphicon-edit"></i>
        </a>
            </td>
            <td>
        <a>
            <i (click)="delete(user.id,user.data.name)" class="glyphicon
                                        glyphicon-remove"></i>
        </a>
        </td>
        </tr>
    </tbody>
</table>
```

users.component.ts

In users.component.ts, we implement the *delete()* method as shown below.

```
delete(userId,name){
  if (confirm("Are you sure you want to delete " + name + "?")){
      this.afs.doc('users/'+userId).delete();
  }
}
```

In the *delete()* method, we first display a confirmation box asking for confirmation to delete. If true, we call the *delete()* method of *this.afs.doc*

```
        this.afs.doc('users/'+userId).delete()
```

The *doc()* method allows us to get one single specific document from firebase. We need to specify the location of the data in firebase as argument to *doc()*. In this case, the location of the object is contained in the 'users' collection with document id. The user id is a unique key is generated for us by firebase whenever we add a document to firebase. The whole idea is to use this unique key to retrieve the object for deletion, and also later for retrieval and update.

Having specified the targeted object using *doc()*, we call the *delete()* method to remove it from firebase.

12.7 Populating the Form on Edit

Having implemented, list, add and delete, we will now implement edit. But before we can implement edit,

161

we need to retrieve the existing requested user document and populate it on the form first. When a user clicks on the **Edit** icon, she would be navigated to the User Form with the given user details populated in the input fields. We also change the title of the page to **Edit User** instead of **Add User**. And if we access the User Form via the Add User button, title should be **New User**.

First in app.routing.ts, we define a new route *add/:id* with *id* being a parameter as shown below. *id* will contain our user object id used to retrieve our *user* object and populate the Edit form.

app.routing.ts

```
import { RouterModule } from '@angular/router';
import { UsersComponent } from './users.component';
import { UserFormComponent } from './user-form.component';

export const routing = RouterModule.forRoot([
    { path:'', component:UsersComponent },
    { path:'add',component:UserFormComponent },
    { path:'add/:id', component: UserFormComponent }
]);
```

users.component.html

Next, in users.component.html, we add the router link to the **Edit** icon with the parameter *user.id* used to retrieve our *user* document and populate our form.

```
        <a [routerLink]="['/add', user.id]">
            <i class="glyphicon glyphicon-edit"></i>
        </a>
```

user-form.component.ts

Next in user-form.component.ts, add the codes below in **bold**.

```
import { Component } from '@angular/core';
import { FormBuilder, FormGroup, Validators } from '@angular/forms';
import { Router, ActivatedRoute } from '@angular/router';
import { AngularFirestore, AngularFirestoreDocument} from 'angularfire2/firestore';

import { User } from './user';
import { Observable } from 'rxjs';

@Component({
    selector:'user-form',
```

```typescript
    templateUrl: 'user-form.component.html'
})
export class UserFormComponent  {
    id;
    form: FormGroup;
    title: string;
    user = new User();

    userDoc: AngularFirestoreDocument<User>;
    singleUser: Observable<User>;

    constructor(fb: FormBuilder, private _router:Router,
private afs: AngularFirestore, private _route:ActivatedRoute){
        this.form = fb.group({
            username:['',Validators.required ],
            email:['',Validators.required]
        })
    }

    ngOnInit(){
        this._route.params.subscribe(params => {
            this.id = params["id"];
        });

        if(!this.id){
            this.title = "New User";
        }
        else{
            this.title = "Edit User";
            this.userDoc = this.afs.doc('users/'+this.id);
            this.singleUser = this.userDoc.valueChanges();
            this.singleUser.subscribe((user) =>{
                this.form.get('username').setValue(user.name);
                this.form.get('email').setValue(user.email);
            });
        }
    }

    submit(){
        this.afs.collection('users').add({
            name: this.user.name,
            email: this.user.email
        });
        this._router.navigate(['']);
    }
}
```

163

Code Explanation

```
import { Router, ActivatedRoute } from '@angular/router';
```

We import *ActivatedRoute* and inject it in our constructor. This is used to retrieve the parameter *id* passed in from User component as shown below.

```
ngOnInit(){
    this._route.params.subscribe(params => {
        this.id = params["id"];
    });

    if(!this.id){
        this.title = "New User";
    }
    else{
        this.title = "Edit User";
        this.userDoc = this.afs.doc('users/'+this.id);
        this.singleUser = this.userDoc.valueChanges();
        this.singleUser.subscribe((user) =>{
            this.form.get('username').setValue(user.name);
            this.form.get('email').setValue(user.email);
        });
    }
}
```

We retrieve *id* from *_route.params* and if it is null, it means that we arrive at UserForm without a parameter and want to perform adding a new user. We thus set the title to "New User".

If *id* is not null, it means we want to edit a user of that given id and therefore display title as "Edit User". We then proceed to retrieve the user object with the below code:

```
this.userDoc = this.afs.doc('users/'+this.id);
this.singleUser.subscribe((user) =>{
    this.form.get('username').setValue(user.name);
    this.form.get('email').setValue(user.email);
});
```

We retrieve a specific user document with *afs.doc* and assign it to *userDoc* of type *AngularFirestoreDocument<User>*. We then call *userDoc.valueChanges()* which returns an Observable which we assign to *singleUser*. We subscribe to *singleUser* which returns us our requested user object in a call back.

```
this.form.get('username').setValue(user.name);
this.form.get('email').setValue(user.email);
```

When we have our requested user object, we then assign the user values to the *username* and *email* form field values to populate our edit form.

12.7 Updating a User

Finally to update the user, we make some code changes and additions to *submit()* in user-form.component.ts. Fill in the below code into *submit()*.

user-form.component.ts

```
submit(){
    if (this.id) {
        this.afs.doc('users/'+this.id).update({
            name: this.user.name,
            email: this.user.email
        });    ;
    }
    else{
        this.afs.collection('users').add({
            name: this.user.name,
            email: this.user.email
        });
    }
    this._router.navigate(['']);
}
```

Code Explanation

We first check if there is an *id*, which means the form is in edit mode. If so, we call the update method of *afs.doc* to *update*. Else, which means the form is in Add New User mode, we call *add()* of *afs.collection* to add the new user object to firebase.

Running your App

If you run your app now, your app should have full functionality to create, update, delete and read user data from and to firebase.

Summary

In this chapter, we learnt how to implement C.R.U.D. operations using Firebase as our backend. We learnt how to add firebase to our application, how to work with the firebase database from the firebase console, how to display a list of users, how to add a user with the *add* method, how to delete a user with the *delete* method, retrieve a single firebase document to prepare our form for edit and how to update a user.

CHAPTER 13: AUTHENTICATION IN FIREBASE

In this chapter, we will learn how to first authenticate users before they can view or edit any data. We will be adding a navigator bar to our app from chapter 12 with login, signup and logout links (fig. 13.0.1). If a user is logged out, he will not be able to access the list of users unless he logins or signs up for an account.

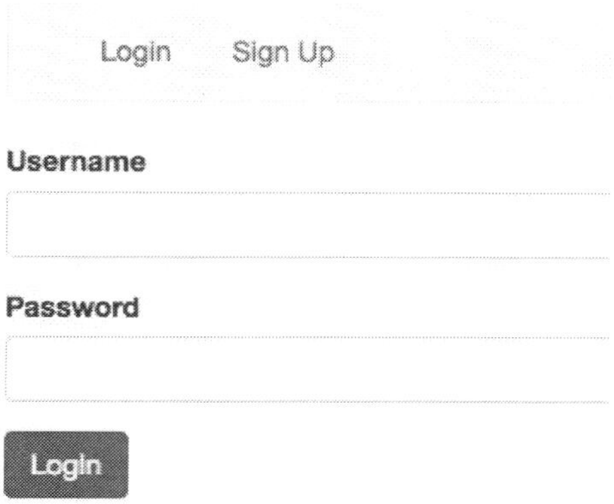

figure 13.0.1

Once a user is logged in, they can then access the list of users (fig. 13.0.2). Logged in users should only see the logout link in the navigation bar and logged out users should see only the login and signup links.

Logout

Users

Add

Username	Email
Greg Lim	greglim@support.com
Jason	jason@lim.com

figure 13.0.2

13.1 Adding Login Component and Login Service

In the existing project from chapter 12, we will start by adding a new login page. We will use the login form from chapter seven. Add the files: login.component.html, login.component.ts and login.service.ts, passwordValidator.ts from chapter 7 (refer to https://github.com/greglim81/angular-chapter7 if you do not already have the source files) into your project *app* folder from chapter 12 (fig. 13.1.1).

figure 13.1.1

Next, import LoginComponent and LoginService into *declaration* and *providers* array of app.module.ts respectively with the following codes in **bold**:

app.module.ts
```
...
import { LoginComponent } from './login.component';
import { LoginService } from './login.service';
...
@NgModule({
  declarations: [
    AppComponent,
    UsersComponent,
    UserFormComponent,
    LoginComponent,
  ],
  imports: [
    BrowserModule,
    AngularFireModule.initializeApp(config),
    AngularFirestoreModule,
    ReactiveFormsModule,
    routing
  ],
```

```
  providers: [LoginService],
  bootstrap: [AppComponent]
})
```

13.2 Firebase Authentication

To implement authentication, we first need to enable authentication for our app in the firebase console. In firebase console, Go to *Authentication*, *Sign-In Method* and enable *'Email and Password'* sign-in provider (fig. 13.2.1).

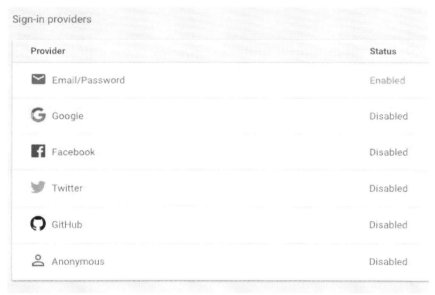

figure 13.2.1

We next have to configure our database rules such that only authenticated users can access our data.

Configuring Database Rules

Our database rules are currently set as:

```
// Allow read/write access on all documents
// to any user signed in to the application

service cloud.firestore {
  match /databases/{database}/documents {
    match /{document=**} {
      allow read, write;
```

```
      }
    }
}
```

This means that anyone can read or write to our database. To implement authentication login and signup, we should now change our rules back to the default for authentication:

```
service cloud.firestore {
  match /databases/{database}/documents {
    match /{document=**} {
      allow read, write: if request.auth.uid != null;
    }
  }
}
```

(note that whenever you change rules in firebase console, you need to 'publish' to apply it)

Our database rule now allows full read and write access to only authenticated users of our app. Which is to say, our *users* or *user* data is not visible to users who are not logged in.

Back in our code, we next need to import *AngularFireAuthModule* in App module. *AngularFireAuthModule* is the individual authentication module in *AngularFire* that we need to add. Add the lines in **bold** below to app.module.ts.

app.module.ts

```
...
import { AngularFireAuthModule } from 'angularfire2/auth';
...
  imports: [
    BrowserModule,
    AngularFireModule.initializeApp(config),
    AngularFirestoreModule,
    ReactiveFormsModule,
    routing,
    AngularFireAuthModule
  ],
...
```

login.service.ts

Our current login method in Login Service from chapter seven is a hardcoded string comparison which is obviously inadequate for authentication.

```
login(username, password){
    if(username === "jason" && password === "123")
        return true;
    else
        return false;
}
```

Instead, implement login.service.ts as shown below:

```
import {Injectable} from '@angular/core';

import {AngularFireAuth} from 'angularfire2/auth';
import {Router} from '@angular/router';
import {BehaviorSubject} from 'rxjs';

@Injectable()
export class LoginService {

  private loggedIn = new BehaviorSubject<boolean>(false);

  constructor( private router:Router,private afAuth: AngularFireAuth){
  }

  get isLoggedIn(){
    return this.loggedIn.asObservable();
  }

  login(username, password){
    if(username !== '' && password !== ''){
        return this.afAuth.auth.signInWithEmailAndPassword(username,password)
            .then(authState => {
                console.log("Login-then",authState);
                this.loggedIn.next(true);

                this.router.navigate(['/']);
            })
            .catch(
                error => {
                    this.router.navigate(['login/' + error.message]);
                    console.log(error);
                }
            );
    }
  }

  logout(){
    this.loggedIn.next(false);
    this.afAuth.auth.signOut();
    this.router.navigate(['/login']);
  }
}
```

Code Explanation

```
login(username, password){
  if(username !== '' && password !== ''){
    return this.afAuth.auth.signInWithEmailAndPassword(username,password)
      ...
}
```

In the *login()* method, we import, inject (in constructor) and call the **AngularFireAuth** library's *signInWithEmailAndPassword* which asynchronously signs in using the provided email and password.

```
.then(authState => {
    console.log("Login-then",authState);
    this.loggedIn.next(true);

    this.router.navigate(['/']);
})
```

If the signin is successful, we proceed to the *then* clause which sets *loggedIn.next(true)* and calls `this.router.navigate(['/'])` to route to the main page. *loggedIn* is a variable of type *BehaviorSubject* as declared in our class:

```
private loggedIn = new BehaviorSubject<boolean>(false);
```

We use *loggedIn* to represent if a user is logged in or not. *loggedIn* is of type *BehaviorSubject* which keeps the latest login boolean status cached. Observers subscribe to it to receive the last emitted login status. When the login is successful, we emit that the user is now logged in (by setting the value in *loggedIn* to true) and redirects the routing to the main page of users.

```
.catch(
    error => {
        this.router.navigate(['login/' + error.message]);
        console.log(error);
    }
);
```

If the sign in fails (e.g. email address is badly formatted, or email and password do not match), we then navigate back to the login form and pass along an error message parameter with the error message to be rendered to the user.

```
logout(){
  this.loggedIn.next(false);
  this.afAuth.auth.signOut();
  this.router.navigate(['/login']);
}
```

When the user logs out of our application, we emit that the user is no longer logged in (by setting the value in *loggedIn* to false), calls *afAuth.auth.signOut()* and redirects to the login page.

```
get isLoggedIn(){
   return this.loggedIn.asObservable();
}
```

In the above getter method, we also expose *loggedIn* as an Observable so that when an Observer subscribes to *isLoggedIn()*, the latest cached *loggedIn* value will be emitted. We will revisit the usage of *isLoggedIn* in the following sections e.g. rendering of navigation bar, route guards etc.

login.component.ts

Next in login.component.ts, we want to show the error message to the user in the login form if there is an invalid login. Add the codes in **bold**.

```
import { Component } from '@angular/core';
import { FormBuilder, FormGroup, Validators } from '@angular/forms';

import { PasswordValidator } from './passwordValidator';
import { LoginService } from './login.service';
import { ActivatedRoute } from '@angular/router';

@Component({
    selector:'login',
    templateUrl: 'login.component.html'
})
export class LoginComponent   {

    form: FormGroup;
    invalidLoginMessage;

    constructor(fb: FormBuilder, private _loginService: LoginService,    private
_route:ActivatedRoute){

        this.form = fb.group({
            username:['',Validators.required ],
             password:['',Validators.compose([Validators.required,
                                  PasswordValidator.cannotContainSpace])]
        })
    }

    ngOnInit(){
        this._route.params.subscribe(params => {
            this.invalidLoginMessage = params["invalidLoginMessage"];
        });
    }

    login(){
```

```
        var result = this._loginService.login(this.form.controls['username'].value,
                            this.form.controls['password'].value);
    }
}
```

We import *ActivatedRoute* and in *ngOnInit*, we retrieve the *invalidLoginMessage* parameter in n*gOnInit()* if it is thrown by Login Service upon unsuccessful login as implemented earlier.

Adding Login to our Routes

We next edit app.routing.ts to add the routes for Login component and *invalidLoginMessage*. Add the codes below in **bold**:

app.routing.ts

```
import { RouterModule } from '@angular/router';
import { UsersComponent } from './users.component';
import { UserFormComponent } from './user-form.component';
import { LoginComponent } from './login.component';

export const routing = RouterModule.forRoot([
    { path:'', component:UsersComponent },
    { path:'add', component:UserFormComponent },
    { path:'add/:id', component: UserFormComponent },
    { path:'login', component:LoginComponent },
    { path:'login/:invalidLoginMessage', component:LoginComponent }
]);
```

Testing our Authentication in the Console

Now run your app and navigate to http://localhost:4200/login. In the login form, login with an invalid email as username, and you should get the below error message logged in the console:

code: "auth/invalid-email", message: "The email address is badly formatted."

Or if you login with an invalid account, you get the below error:

code: "auth/user-not-found", message: "There is no user record corresponding to this identifier. The user may have been deleted."

At this point, we have not implemented our sign up function yet to create any user accounts. But you can create a user account directly in firebase console. Proceed to create a test user like in fig. 13.2.2.

figure 13.2.2

Once you have created your test user in firebase console, try logging in again with the user credentials and you should be able to login successfully with something like (logged in console):

Login-then vk {B: Array(0), G: "AIzaSyBFn-c8pyMoTxeEOK/IZpFbeaT/HW4raAY", s: "[DEFAULT]", w: "firestore-50589.firebaseapp.com", c: oh, …}

We should emphasize that when a user signs in successfully, they are then directed to the home page. This is because we have already previously implemented this in our Login Service:

```
login(username, password){
    if(username !== '' && password !== ''){
        return this.afAuth.auth.signInWithEmailAndPassword(username,password)
            .then(authState => {
                console.log("Login-then",authState);
                this.loggedIn.next(true);
                this.router.navigate(['/']);
            })
```

Rendering Invalid Message Alert in Login Form

Currently, we are just logging the error messages to the console. Now, we want to show the invalid login error message in the login form when the login fails (fig.13.2.3).

175

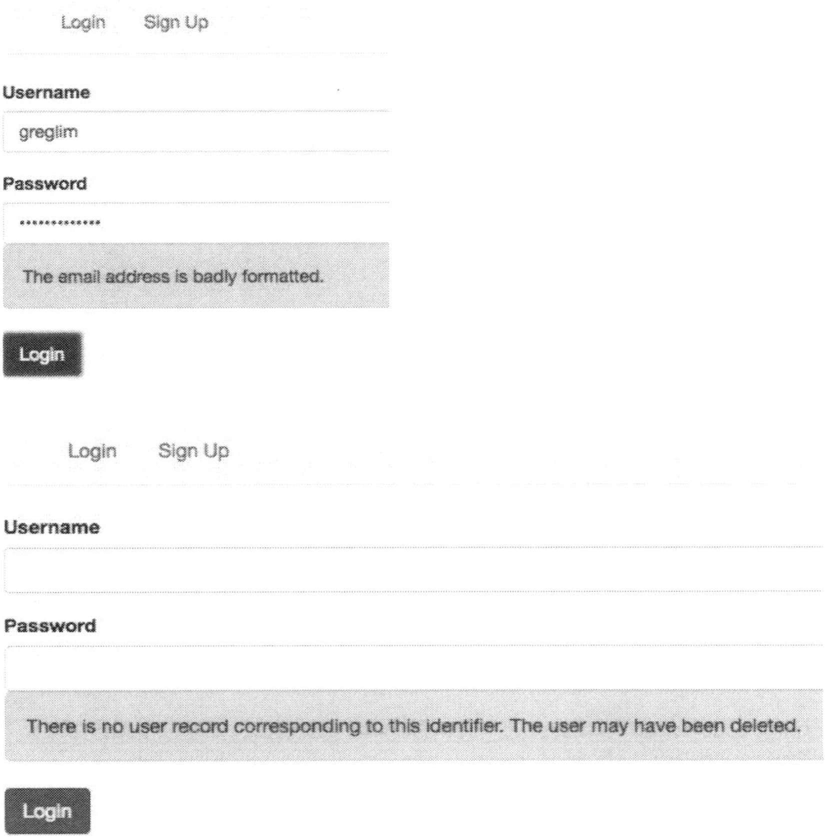

Login   Sign Up

Username

greglim

Password

••••••••••••

The email address is badly formatted.

Login

Login   Sign Up

Username

Password

There is no user record corresponding to this identifier. The user may have been deleted.

Login

figure 13.2.3

In login.component.html, add the codes in **bold** shown below:

login.component.html

```
<form [formGroup]="form" (ngSubmit)="login()">
    <div class="form-group">
        <label for="username">Username</label>
        <input type="text" class="form-control" formControlName="username">
        <div *ngIf="form.controls.username.touched
                && !form.controls.username.valid" class="alert alert-danger">
            Username is required
        </div>
    </div>
    <div class="form-group">
    <label for="password">Password</label>
    <input type="password" class="form-control" formControlName="password">
```

176

```
    <div *ngIf="form.controls.password.touched && form.controls.password.errors">
        <div *ngIf="form.controls.password.errors.invalidLogin"
class="alert alert-danger">
            Username or password is invalid.
        </div>
        <div *ngIf="form.controls.password.errors.required"
class="alert alert-danger">
            Password is required.
        </div>
        <div *ngIf="form.controls.password.errors.cannotContainSpace"
class="alert alert-danger">
            Password cannot contain space.
        </div>
    </div>
    <div *ngIf="invalidLoginMessage" class="alert alert-danger">
        {{invalidLoginMessage}}
    </div>
</div>

    <button class="btn btn-primary" type="submit">Login</button>
</form>
```

The *<div *ngIf>* section we have added in the login form checks if *invalidLoginMessage* consists of any string value, and renders the string value as the error alert to the form. Else *invalidLoginMessage* would be null, which means that the login is successful and we don't have to render any error login message.

We have completed our Login page. Next, we will implement our Sign Up page.

13.3 Sign Up Page

Let's begin creating our Signup component. The codes for our Signup component will be similar to our Login component.

Create a new file signup.component.ts and copy contents from login.component.ts. In signup.component.ts, make sure that you change the class name to *SignupComponent* and replace *login()* method with the following code:

```
onSignup(){
   var result = this._loginService.signup(
            this.form.controls['username'].value,
            this.form.controls['password'].value);
}
```

signup.component.html

Likewise, signup.component.html will be very similar to login.component.html with username and password fields. Copy the code from login.component.html and paste it into signup.component.html and change the codes shown in **bold** below.

```
<form [formGroup]="form" (ngSubmit)="onSignup()">
    <div class="form-group">
        <label for="username">Username</label>
        <input type="text" class="form-control" formControlName="username">
        <div *ngIf="form.controls.username.touched
                && !form.controls.username.valid" class="alert alert-danger">
            Username is required
        </div>
    </div>
    <div class="form-group">
    <label for="password">Password</label>
    <input type="password" class="form-control" formControlName="password">
    <div *ngIf="form.controls.password.touched && form.controls.password.errors">
        <div *ngIf="form.controls.password.errors.required"
class="alert alert-danger">
            Password is required.
        </div>
        <div *ngIf="form.controls.password.errors.cannotContainSpace"
class="alert alert-danger">
            Password cannot contain space.
        </div>
    </div>
    <div *ngIf="invalidLoginMessage" class="alert alert-danger">
            {{invalidLoginMessage}}
    </div>
</div>

    <button class="btn btn-primary" type="submit">Sign Up</button>
</form>
```

login.service.ts

Next in Login Service, add the following *signup* method.

```
  signup(username: string, password: string){
    return
this.afAuth.auth.createUserWithEmailAndPassword(username,password)
        .then(
            authState => {
                console.log("signup-then",authState);
                this.loggedIn.next(true);
                this.router.navigate(['/']);
            }
        )
```

```
    .catch(
        error => {
            var errorMessage = error.message;
            this.router.navigate(['signup/' + error.message]);
            console.log(error);
        }
    );
}
```

You will notice that our *signup* method in LoginService is similar to the *login* method except that *signup()* calls `afAuth.auth.createUserWithEmailAndPassword`.

`createUserWithEmailAndPassword` encodes our data and sends it to a RESTful API on the Firebase Google server to create a user for us. If the sign up is successful, we set *loggedIn* to true and navigate to the main *users* page. Else, navigate back to the signup page with the error message as route parameter.

If the sign up is successful, you can check for the newly created user in the firebase console authentication users list (fig. 13.3.1).

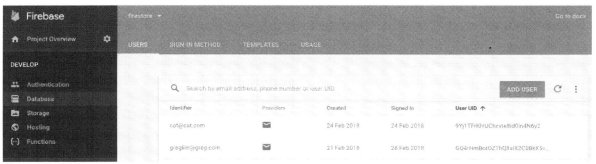

figure 13.3.1

app.routing.ts

Just as we have specified our routes for Login Component, we have to do the same for Signup as well. In app.routing.ts, add the codes shown below:

```
import { RouterModule } from '@angular/router';
import { UsersComponent } from './users.component';
import { UserFormComponent } from './user-form.component';
import { LoginComponent } from './login.component';
import { SignupComponent } from './signup.component';
```

179

```
export const routing = RouterModule.forRoot([
    { path:'', component:UsersComponent },
    { path:'add',component:UserFormComponent },
    { path:'add/:id', component: UserFormComponent },
    { path:'login',component:LoginComponent },
    { path:'login/:invalidLoginMessage',component:LoginComponent },
    { path:'signup',component:SignupComponent },
    { path:'signup/:invalidLoginMessage',component:SignupComponent }
]);
```

We also have to import and declare Signup Component to App Module as shown in bold below.

app.module.ts

```
...
import { SignupComponent } from './signup.component';
...
@NgModule({
  declarations: [
    AppComponent,
    UsersComponent,
    UserFormComponent,
    LoginComponent,
    SignupComponent
  ],
```

Running your App

When you run your app now, navigate to http://localhost:4200/signup and sign up as a new user. This new user will be reflected in the firebase console - *Authentication*, under *Users*.

And if you try signing up with the same email address twice, you get the following error message:

Now that we have completed our Login and Signup pages, let's proceed on to Authentication Guards.

13.4 AuthGuards

In this section, we implement our route guard to prevent access to certain pages unless a user is signed in. Create a new file auth.guard.ts with the following code:

auth.guard.ts

```
import { Injectable } from '@angular/core';
import { CanActivate, ActivatedRouteSnapshot,RouterStateSnapshot, Router} from
'@angular/router';
import { LoginService } from './login.service';
import { Observable } from 'rxjs';
//import 'rxjs/add/operator/take';
//import 'rxjs/add/operator/map';
import { take,map } from 'rxjs/operators';

@Injectable()
export class AuthGuard implements CanActivate {
    constructor(private loginService: LoginService, private router:Router){

    }

    canActivate(next:ActivatedRouteSnapshot,state: RouterStateSnapshot)
      :Observable<boolean>{
        return this.loginService.isLoggedIn
            .pipe(take(1),
               map((isLoggedIn:boolean) => {
                 if(!isLoggedIn){
                    this.router.navigate(['/login']);
                    return false;
                 }
```

```
            return true;
        })
    }
}
```

In the *canActivate* interface method, we return a boolean Observable. *canActivate* will be called by the route guard which waits for the Observable to resolve and check if *isLoggedIn* emits *true*. The *take(1)* Observable operator ensures that *isLoggedIn* emits only the first item and completes because we are only interested in checking the logged in Boolean value from the Observable a single time.

If the user is not logged in, we navigate to the login page and return false to restrict access to the requested page. Else it means that the user is logged and we return true thus allowing the user to access the requested page.

Having implemented the Auth Guard, we then apply it to our routes in app.routing.ts as shown below in bold.

app.routing.ts

```
import { RouterModule } from '@angular/router';
import { UsersComponent } from './users.component';
import { UserFormComponent } from './user-form.component';
import { LoginComponent } from './login.component';
import { SignupComponent } from './signup.component';
import { AuthGuard } from './auth.guard';

export const routing = RouterModule.forRoot([
    { path:'', component:UsersComponent, canActivate:[AuthGuard] },
    { path:'add',component:UserFormComponent, canActivate:[AuthGuard]},
    { path:'add/:id', component: UserFormComponent, canActivate:[AuthGuard] },
    { path:'login',component:LoginComponent },
    { path:'login/:invalidLoginMessage',component:LoginComponent },
    { path:'signup',component:SignupComponent },
    { path:'signup/:invalidLoginMessage',component:SignupComponent }
]);
```

Note that the route guard is only applied to the main, add and edit users page. The login and signup pages do not have any guards applied.

Do remember to import and specify Auth Guard in *providers* of app.module.ts as shown below.

app.module.ts

```
...
import { AuthGuard } from './auth.guard';
```

182

```
...
providers: [LoginService,AuthGuard],
```

13.5 Managing the User State.

Now, we want an already authenticated user to go straight to the main page instead of having to login each time they open the app. To do this, we implement *getCurrentUser* in login.service.ts as shown below:

```
getCurrentUser(){
    return this.afAuth.authState.subscribe(authState => {
        if(authState){
            this.loggedIn.next(true);
            this.router.navigate(['/']);

            console.log("logged in as " + authState.uid);
        }
        else{
            this.router.navigate(['login']);
        }
    });
}
```

afAuth.authState returns an *Observable<firebase.User>* to monitor our application's authentication state if there is a logged in user. We subscribe to *authState* and if *authState* exists, we set *loggedIn* to true and navigate to the main page. Else if it is null, it means the user has been logged out and we navigate to the Login page.

Next, we call *getCurrentUser* from app.component.ts, by adding the following codes in **bold**.

app.component.ts

```
import { Component } from '@angular/core';
import { LoginService } from './login.service';

@Component({
  selector: 'app-root',
  template: `
    <router-outlet></router-outlet>
  `
})
export class AppComponent {

  constructor(private loginService: LoginService){
  }

  ngOnInit(){
```

```
      this.loginService.getCurrentUser();
    }
  }
```

We import Login Service, get an instance by injecting it in the constructor and in *ngOnInit*, we call *loginService.getCurrentUser* so that an already authenticated user goes straight to the main page instead of having to login each time they open the app.

13.6 Displaying our App Navigation Header

Next, we want to display a header with login and sign up links if a user is not logged in (fig. 13.6.1).

Login   Sign Up

Username

greglim

figure 13.6.1

And for logged in users, we display only the logout link (fig. 13.6.2).

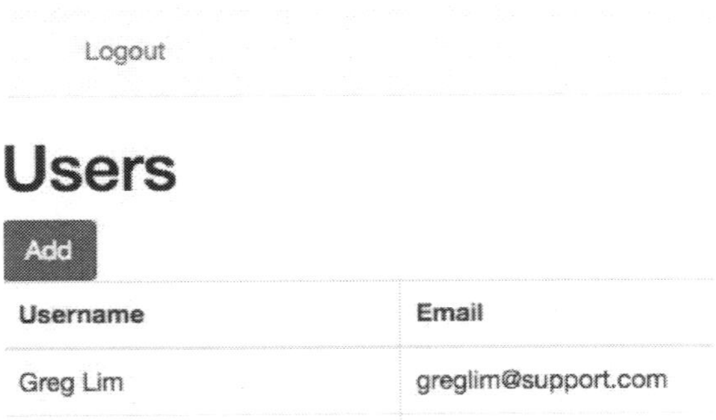

Logout

Users

Add

Username	Email
Greg Lim	greglim@support.com

figure 13.6.2

To do so, in app.component.ts add the following codes in **bold**:

```
import { Component } from '@angular/core';
import { LoginService } from './login.service';
import { Observable } from 'rxjs';

@Component({
  selector: 'app-root',
  template: `
```

184

```
      <nav class="navbar navbar-default">
      <div class="container-fluid">
        <div class="collapse navbar-collapse" id="bs-example-navbar-collapse-1">
          <ul class="nav navbar-nav">
              <li><a (click)="onLogout()" *ngIf="isLoggedIn | async">Logout</a></li>
              <li><a routerLink="login" *ngIf="!(isLoggedIn | async)">Login</a></li>
              <li><a    routerLink="signup"    *ngIf="!(isLoggedIn    |    async)">Sign
Up</a></li>
          </ul>
        </div><!-- /.navbar-collapse -->
      </div><!-- /.container-fluid -->
      </nav>
      <router-outlet></router-outlet>
  `
})
export class AppComponent {
  isLoggedIn: Observable<boolean>;

  constructor(private loginService: LoginService){
  }

  ngOnInit(){
    this.loginService.getCurrentUser();
    this.isLoggedIn = this.loginService.isLoggedIn;
  }

  onLogout(){
    this.loginService.logout();
  }

}
```

Code Explanation

In the template of App Component, we display a template with a modified navigation bar template from *getbootstrap*. We have three links Logout, Login and Sign Up as rendered in the template:

```
<li><a (click)="onLogout()" *ngIf="isLoggedIn | async">Logout</a></li>
<li><a routerLink="login" *ngIf="!(isLoggedIn | async)">Login</a></li>
<li><a routerLink="signup" *ngIf="!(isLoggedIn | async)">Sign Up</a></li>
```

The Logout link calls the onLogout() method which in turn calls the logout() method in Login Service. Using *ngIf*, we show the Logout link only when *isLoggedIn* is true. Note that we need to apply the *async* pipe as *isLoggedIn* is an Observable which emits Boolean values. Remember that the *async* pipe subscribes/unsubscribes to/from the Observable automatically and is considered a best practise by the Angular community.

Conversely, we show the Login and Sign Up links with their router links when *isLoggedIn* is not true.

185

Running our App

If we run our app now and if we are logged in, we will be brought directly to the home page. If you click logout, you will be logged out and brought to the login page. And when you reload this time around, you will be brought to the login page since you have already logged out.

13.7 How Firebase Authenticates

Now that we have completed the Login functionality, let's now understand the mechanics of how Firebase provides authentication in our Angular app.

Authentication in our Angular app and firebase happens by we first sending authentication credentials (email, password) to the server. The server checks the credentials if they are valid and generates a token and return this token to the client. The client stores this token and on each request to a protected resource on the server, it will resend the token to the server. The token proves that a client has already authenticated with the server some time ago and the server can check if it's valid. If the token is valid, the client will request the server to provide access to whatever protected resource the client is trying to access. Naturally, such tokens also invalidate after a couple of minutes or hours. This is the approach used internally by firebase in our Angular apps.

If we run our app in the browser, we can see that firebase stores the token in *Local Storage* of browser. If you go to 'Chrome developer tools', 'Application', 'Storage', 'Local Storage', 'localhost:4200' (figure…), you can see the key and value of the generated token.

Initially before we login, there are no key-value pairs (fig. 13.7.1).

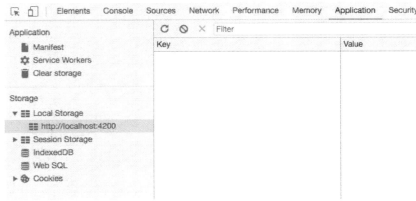

figure 13.7.1

If you login now, you will see a new key-value pair token generated (fig. 13.7.2):

figure 13.7.2

And if you logout, the token is deleted.

Summary

In this chapter, we learnt how to implement authentication using Firebase in our app. We added a login page, a sign up page, and an authentication Login service to our project. Hopefully, we should now have a better understanding of how to implement authentication using firebase authentication.

You can access the full code for this chapter at https://github.com/greglim81/angular-chapter13

CHAPTER 14: IMPLEMENTING FOR MULTIPLE USERS

Currently, all authenticated users access the set same of data and this is certainly what we do not want. Who wants other people to be looking at your data? And who is interested in looking at others' data (unless you are a spy!). In this chapter, we will improve our application such that each user access their own data.

Firestore Collection and Documents for Multiple Users

In Firestore, we currently have a root *users* collection which contains *user* documents. To allow for multiple users, we should change our Firestore data structure like:

--users collection
   --user1 document
     --clients collection
       --clientA
       --clientB
   --user2 document
     --clients collection
       --clientA
       --clientB

*Note that the term *collection* and *document* are key terms in the Firestore documentation which you can find out more at (https://cloud.google.com/firestore/docs/).

The root *users* collection is now referring to the collection of users of our application. Each user of the *users* collection e.g. user1, user2 is a document. Each user document would then further contain a *client* collection which stores the set of *client* documents for that user. To avoid confusion if it's a user of our application, or a user's users data, I have changed user's users data to user's clients data. We call the *clients* collection as a subcollection. A subcollection is a collection associated with a specific document in our case *user*.

With this data structure, each user will only have access to his own *clients* collection. Do you see a pattern of collection, document, collection, document? Collections and documents must always follow this pattern. You cannot reference a collection in a collection or a document in a document. Find out more about collections and documents at https://firebase.google.com/docs/firestore/data-model.

Implementing Multiple Users in Code

The main change to our code is that we have to include the current logged in user id whenever we execute a create, read, update or delete operation.

Firstly, we have to retrieve the current logged in user id. We essentially retrieve the current logged in user id when we sign in, sign up or get current user. To do so, in login.service.ts, add the code changes in **bold**:

login.service.ts

```
...
export class LoginService {

  private loggedIn = new BehaviorSubject<boolean>(false);
  loggedInUser;

  ...

  login(username, password){
    if(username !== '' && password !== ''){
      return
this.afAuth.auth.signInWithEmailAndPassword(username,password)
        .then(authState => {
          console.log("Login-then",authState);
          this.loggedIn.next(true);
          this.loggedInUser=authState.uid;
          this.router.navigate(['/']);
        })
        .catch(
          ...
        );
    }
  }

  logout(){
    this.loggedIn.next(false);
    this.afAuth.auth.signOut();
    this.loggedInUser=null;
    this.router.navigate(['/login']);
  }

  signup(username: string, password: string){
    return
this.afAuth.auth.createUserWithEmailAndPassword(username,password)
        .then(
          authState => {
            console.log("signup-then",authState);
            this.loggedIn.next(true);
```

190

```
                this.loggedInUser=authState.uid;
                this.router.navigate(['/']);
            }
        )
        .catch(
            ...
        );
    }

    getCurrentUser(){
        return this.afAuth.authState.subscribe(authState => {
            if(authState){
                this.loggedIn.next(true);
                this.loggedInUser=authState.uid;
                this.router.navigate(['/']);
                console.log("logged in as " + authState.uid);
            }
            else{
                this.router.navigate(['login']);
            }
        });
    }


}
```

We have a variable *loggedInUser* to store the current logged in user. In the *login*, *signup* and *getCurrentUser* methods, we assign *authState.uid* to *loggedInUser*. Also, in *logout*, we set *loggedInUser* to null to represent that there is no user currently logged in.

Next in user-form.component.ts, make the following changes:

user-form.component.ts

```
...
import {LoginService} from './login.service';

...
export class UserFormComponent  {
    ...

    constructor(fb: FormBuilder, private _router:Router,
        private afs: AngularFirestore, private _route:ActivatedRoute,
        private _loginService: LoginService){
        ...
    }
```

```
...
ngOnInit(){
    this._route.params.subscribe(params => {
        this.id = params["id"];
    });

    if(!this.id){
        this.title = "New User";
    }
    else{
        this.title = "Edit User";
        this.userDoc = this.afs.doc('users/'+
          this._loginService.loggedInUser+"/clients/"+this.id);
        this.singleUser = this.userDoc.valueChanges();
        this.singleUser.subscribe((user) =>{
            this.form.get('username').setValue(user.name);
            this.form.get('email').setValue(user.email);
        });
    }
}

submit(){
    if (this.id) {
        this.afs.doc('users/'+this._loginService.loggedInUser+
          "/clients/"+this.id).update({
            name: this.user.name,
            email: this.user.email
        });    ;
    }
    else{
        this.afs.collection("users")
          .doc(this._loginService.loggedInUser)
          .collection("clients").add({
            name: this.user.name,
            email: this.user.email
        });
    }
    this._router.navigate(['']);
}
}
```

Code Explanation

In user-form.component.ts, we include the logged in user id and append it to the document location in *ngOnInit*:

192

```
this.userDoc = this.afs.doc('users/'+
  this._loginService.loggedInUser+"/clients/"+this.id);
```

The above code retrieves the existing client document data to populate it in the form.

We similarly include the logged in user id to the client document location to update an existing client document in *submit()*:

```
this.afs.doc('users/'+this._loginService.loggedInUser+
  "/clients/"+this.id).update({
```

The same applies when we add a client document by doing the following:

```
this.afs.collection("users")
  .doc(this._loginService.loggedInUser)
  .collection("clients").add({
    name: this.user.name,
    email: this.user.email
});
```

We next append the logged in user id to users.component.ts.

users.component.ts

...

```
import { LoginService } from './login.service'; //
```

...

```
export class UsersComponent {

  ...

  constructor(private afs: AngularFirestore, private _router: Router,
private _loginService: LoginService){

  }

  ngOnInit(){
    this.usersCol = this.afs.collection('users/' +
      this._loginService.loggedInUser + '/clients');
    this.users = this.usersCol.snapshotChanges()
      .pipe(
        map(actions => {
          return actions.map( a => {
```

```
                    const data = a.payload.doc.data() as User;
                    const id = a.payload.doc.id;
                    return { id, data};
                });
            })
        );
    }

    add(){
       this._router.navigate(['add']);
    }

    delete(userId,name){
       if (confirm("Are you sure you want to delete " + name + "?")){
          this.afs.doc('users/'+
              this._loginService.loggedInUser+"/clients/"+userId).delete();
       }
    }
}
```

Similar to what we do in User Form component, we retrieve the *loggedInUser* from Login service to access the *loggedInUser* clients collection in *ngOnInit*. We do the same to access the client document in *delete()*.

Running the App

If we run the app now, we find that we can now add, update, delete clients for each specific user. If you create multiple user accounts, each user account can read/write to her own set of clients only. Our app can now enable multiple users to manage their own client list!

Summary

In this chapter, we learnt how to use Firestore sub-collections and documents to cater for multiple users in our app. You can access the full code for this chapter at https://github.com/greglim81/angular-chapter14/

With this knowledge, you can move on and build more complicated enterprise level fully functional Angular applications of your own!

Hopefully, you have enjoyed this book and would like to learn more from me. I would love to get your feedback, learning what you liked and didn't for us to improve.

Please feel free to email me at support@i-ducate.com if you encounter any errors with your code or to get updated versions of this book. Visit my GitHub repository at https://github.com/greglim81 if you have not already to have the full source code for this book.

If you didn't like the book, or if you feel that I should have covered certain additional topics, please email us to let us know. This book can only get better thanks to readers like you.

If you like the book, I would appreciate if you could leave us a review too.

Thank you and all the best for your learning journey in Angular!

ABOUT THE AUTHOR

Greg Lim is a technologist and author of several programming books. Greg has many years in teaching programming in tertiary institutions and he places special emphasis on learning by doing.

Contact Greg at support@i-ducate.com.

Made in the USA
San Bernardino, CA
28 January 2020